Praise for *The Strengths Book*...

...On Inspiring the Best of You

"Alex and his colleagues know how to unlock your strengths better than anyone else on the planet."
David Taylor, Author of *The Naked Leader* books

"*The Strengths Book* provides a call to action for everyone to find what is strongest about themselves and maximise it. The Hall of Fame section for each of the sixty strengths provides a veritable catalogue of male and female role models, which should inspire everyone to make the most of the life that they have been granted."
Marci Shimoff, # 1 *New York Times* bestselling author, *Happy for No Reason* and *Chicken Soup for the Soul*

"Positive psychology has the potential to strengthen the world. A major challenge is taking robust theories and making them accessible, practical and useful. This book delivers on all counts. I thought it was fab. I am ordering copies for academics, practitioners and people who are simply interested."
Sebastian Bailey, Co-founder, The Mind Gym

"The most extraordinary thing I've learnt about the strengths approach is its universal applicability. *The Strengths Book* is thoughtful and engaging but above all it is deeply practical."
David Robinson OBE, Community Links, & Vice-Chair, Prime Minister's Council on Social Action

"What Obi-Wan Kenobi taught Luke Skywalker, Alex, Janet and Robert teach each and everyone of us in a radical and culture-shifting book. May the force be with you."
Marc Mathieu, Founder of BeDo, former Senior Vice President of Global Brand Marketing, Coca-Cola

"Doing what you do best simply is best. Best for you. Best for your friends, family and loved ones. Best for your colleagues. Even best for your boss! Here's a book,   shows us all why identifying and play   unlock the door to a more fun, energ
Nic Mar

D1316283

Well-being, oundation)

"*The Strengths Book* ushers in the second decade of a century devoted to positive psychology. It combines the deep eastern and western insights of the last centuries and provides a guide for the future..."

Jitendra Mohan, Professor Emeritus of Psychology, Panjab University, Chandigarh, India, and President, Asian Association of Applied Psychology

"It is so easy to focus on our weaknesses and become preoccupied by what we perceive we can't do. This book and the work of CAPP turn that notion on its head and help us identify our strengths and how we can use them to develop our skills and our belief in our own abilities and attitudes."

David Moorcroft MBE & OBE, Point Four One, and 3000m and 5000m UK record holder since July 1982

...On Leading in Organisations

"The strength of *The Strengths Book* lies in its clear description of what strengths are, why they matter, and how to recognise them.... *The Strengths Book* is a well thought through and carefully crafted book by strengths experts who want to strengthen us."

Dave Ulrich, Professor, Ross School of Business, University of Michigan, and Partner, The RBL Group, *BusinessWeek* #1 Management Educator & Guru

"The ability to understand yourself at your best and to be true to this in the moment is the bedrock of truly effective leadership. This excellent book enables both experienced and emerging leaders to appreciate, honour and strengthen their unique capacities, and to harness these to their full potential for the greater good."

Arvinder S. Dhesi, Group Talent Director, Aviva plc

"Meeting and working with the team at CAPP has opened my eyes to the power of strengths, and how focussing on them can improve both the performance and the work experience of teams and individuals."

Mark Rayner, Head of Training and Development, Hampshire Fire and Rescue Service

"More than ever before, organisations who strive for excellence will need to be highly self-aware, understand the power (and fragility) of relationships and develop and equip their leaders to enjoy making their staff stronger, more self-reliant and more productive. *The Strengths Book* helps you navigate that journey."

Tarik Chawdry, Assistant HR Director, Birmingham City Council

"Consciously being aware of one's strengths and analysing strengths in others can lead to great results...It sounds easy and common sense but requires conscious effort... I would urge you to read this book to help your conscious effort become unconscious."
Gifford Tanser, Human Resources Director, Boehringer Ingelheim

"... Developing organisations built around strengths represents just such a shift and *The Strengths Book* offers a route that enables existing assumptions to be challenged and alternative strategies to be deployed."
Nick Barclay, Client Director, Executive Education, Warwick Business School

...On Enabling Happiness and Flourishing

"To identify what really matters in our life, to acknowledge the potential that we all have within ourselves, and to apply joyful effort in actualizing it are some of the essential keys to human flourishing that are so well presented in this inspiring, practical, and meaningful book."
Matthieu Ricard, author of *Happiness: A Guide to Developing Life's Most Important Skill*

"This book lights your unique path to flourishing. Digest it and come alive with positivity and possibility."
Barbara Fredrickson, Ph.D., author of *Positivity: Discover the Groundbreaking Science to Release Your Inner Optimist and Thrive*

"An innovative exhibition of the evidence for appreciating, building, and creating a life that revolves around strength use. If you are interested in dynamic strategies for becoming energized, productive, creative and fully alive, *The Strengths Book* is an essential read..."
Todd B. Kashdan, Ph.D., author of *Curious? Discover the Missing Ingredient to a Fulfilling Life*

"*The Strengths Book* offers a new perspective on the challenge of being, informed by the intellectual and philosophical revolution of positive psychology. Quite simply it offers a pathway to flourishing and growing through both the good and the challenging times in our lives."
Professor Michael West, Executive Dean, Aston Business School

...On Developing Yourself and Others

"This book takes a giant step forward in making an approach to strengths development accessible and useful...an outstanding, practical, and engaging discussion of strengths...I plan on distributing copies to everyone I know."

Kim Cameron, Editor, *Positive Organizational Scholarship*, and William Russell Kelly Professor of Management and Organizations, Ross School of Business, University of Michigan

"A timely and practical book by leaders in the field. If you are looking for a book that helps you to identify and harness your strengths, you've found it."

Susan David, Ph.D., Co-director, Institute of Coaching, McLean/Harvard Medical School

"...*The Strengths Book* is a powerful, practical and pragmatic guide...I thoroughly recommend it to anyone who is interested in discovering and developing the best of themselves and others."

Dr. Anthony Seldon, Master, Wellington College

"... A wonderful field book on the subject, whether you want to know the science behind CAPP's strengths studies, to hear and pass on strengthspotting stories and tips or to have a simple, easy to use compendium of the sixty strengths of Realise2. .."

Steve Chapman, Director of Organisation Development (Manufacturing), GlaxoSmithKline

"The most readable, practical book on strengths that I have yet seen. If you are looking for a more sophisticated and evidence-based approach, if you want to know how to use strengths-based positive psychology more effectively, if you want to get the best out of yourself and others - this is the book for you."

Dr. Anthony M. Grant, Director, Coaching Psychology Unit, University of Sydney, Australia

"Whether you have 'hit a wall' in your career and want to change direction, or if you simply want to pause, take stock and reconsider what you need to do differently in order to flourish where you are, *The Strengths Book* and the Realise2 assessment will prove invaluable resources."

Anne Wilson, Careers Consultant, University of Warwick

"*The Strengths Book* enables us to take pride in and to boost thos areas where we naturally shine, while developing strategies t minimise the impact of our weaknesses rather than to try to be a things to all people. I will be turning to its sound advice repeated in both my business and personal life."

Angela Blacklaw, Head of Talent Developmen
in the Public Sect

"... *The Strengths Book* makes a welcome change by taking a positi\ approach. In combination with the Realise2 strengths assessment, helps you to understand your strengths and how to use them to th benefit of yourself, your team, your department or yo organisation."

Heinz Landau, Executive Vice President Group Strategy ar
Corporate Development, B. Grimm Group, Thailar

"...This book provides the language and practical tools to assess ou strengths as well as bringing it alive with useful case studies... Th *Strengths Book* provides a refreshing, positive and practical guide t assessing and building our strengths."

David Stephenson, Group Head of OD, Royal Mail Grou

"Every ordained Minister should read this book to develop their gif and graces into strengths of ministry."

Revd. Dr. Howard Mellor, Discernment and Selectio
Co-ordinator, The Methodist Churc

The Strengths Book

Be Confident, Be Successful, and Enjoy Better Relationships by Realising the Best of You

Alex Linley
Janet Willars
Robert Biswas-Diener

With contributing authors
Nicky Garcea
Martin Stairs

CAPP PRESS

The Venture Centre
University of Warwick Science Park
Coventry CV4 7EZ
United Kingdom
Tel: +44 (0)24 76 323 363
Fax: +44 (0)24 76 323 001
Email: capp@cappeu.com
Website: www.cappeu.com

CAPP Press is a trading name of the Centre of Applied Positive Psychology Ltd,
registered in England and Wales, company number 06802155

First published in the United Kingdom in 2010

ISBN: 978-1-906366-09-4 (paperback)

British Library Cataloguing-in-Publication Data
A catalogue record for this book is available from the British Library.

Printed in the United Kingdom

10 9 8 7 6 5 4 3 2 1

It is the policy of CAPP Press to use paper from sources that are SFI
(Sustainable Forestry Initiative) and PEFC (Programme for the Endorsement
of Forest Certification Schemes) Certified.

Other books in the CAPP Press *Strengthening the World* series

Average to A+: Realising Strengths in Yourself and Others (2008)
Alex Linley

Celebrating Strengths: Building Strengths-based Schools (2008)
Jennifer M. Fox Eades

Other Books by the Authors

Oxford Handbook of Positive Psychology and Work
Edited by P. Alex Linley, Susan Harrington & Nicola Garcea
Published by Oxford University Press, New York, 2010

Happiness: Unlocking the Mysteries of Psychological Wealth
Ed Diener & Robert Biswas-Diener
Published by Wiley Blackwell, Hoboken, NJ, 2008
2008 Winner of the PROSE Award for Psychology

Trauma, Recovery and Growth: Positive Psychological Perspectives on Posttraumatic Stress
Edited by Stephen Joseph & P. Alex Linley
Published by Wiley, Hoboken, NJ, 2008

Positive Psychology Coaching: Putting the Science of Happiness to Work for Your Clients
Robert Biswas-Diener & Ben Dean
Published by Wiley, Hoboken, NJ, 2007

Positive Therapy: A Meta-Theory for Positive Psychological Practice
Stephen Joseph & P. Alex Linley
Published by Taylor & Francis, London, 2006

Positive Psychology in Practice
Edited by P. Alex Linley & Stephen Joseph
Published by Wiley, Hoboken, NJ, 2004

For those who seek to be strengthened

"All the alchemists played to their strengths. That was one secret of their success."
Charles and Elizabeth Handy, *The New Alchemists*

"Success is achieved by developing our strengths, not by eliminating our weaknesses."
Marilyn vos Savant, Highest IQ in the *Guinness Hall of Fame*

"Throughout my life, I've always needed somebody as a counterbalance, to compensate for my weaknesses, and work off my strengths. Jonny and I were a good team. He knew who we should interview, and why. I had the ability to persuade them to say yes, and the obstinacy never to accept no for an answer."
Richard Branson, *Losing My Virginity*

"Bringing together two or more people with complementary strengths not only compensates for the shortcomings of each but also results in a team in which the whole is much greater than the sum of the parts."
Stephen Miles & Michael Watkins, *Harvard Business Review*

"It is only by combining the strengths of everyone in the organization and helping them to work to his or her best ability that organizations can win in the marketplace today."
Noel Tichy, *The Leadership Engine*

"The unique purpose of organization is to make strength productive."
Peter Drucker, *The Effective Executive*

The Strengths Book in Ten Easy Steps

1 Most of us don't have an accurate understanding of what our strengths are — but through this book we'll show you how to get there.

2 Strengths are the things we are good at AND that energise us. This is the first mistake people make, because traditionally we have thought that our strengths are simply the things we are good at doing.

3 Many of us confuse our Learned Behaviours with our Strengths. If we're good at something, but it drains us to do it, it is a Learned Behaviour.

4 Our Learned Behaviours come about because we get rewarded for doing them — the pat on the head at work, the promotion, the pay rise — all can be things that pull us away from doing what we enjoy and get us doing things well enough but without enjoying them. Using our Learned Behaviours excessively over time, we will burn out.

5 Our strengths can be Realised Strengths, that we get to use regularly, or Unrealised Strengths, that we don't have the opportunity to use so much.

6 Our Unrealised Strengths are our greatest areas for development — not our Weaknesses, as traditional folklore suggests.

7 Our Weaknesses are the things that we are not good at doing and that also drain us. So it's bad news all round when we have to focus on our Weaknesses, as the research evidence shows.

8 As such, the best advice is to:
   - *Marshal your Realised Strengths* — by using them to best effect, but not too much.
   - *Maximise your Unrealised Strengths* — by finding opportunities to use them more.

- *Moderate your Learned Behaviours* — by not using them too much.
- *Minimise your Weaknesses* — by finding ways to stop having to focus on them.

9 We can moderate our Learned Behaviours and minimise our Weaknesses through role shaping, complementary partnering, and strengths-based team working. This book will show you how.

10 There are 60 strengths, from Action to Work Ethic, that are included in this book, and in our online strengths assessment tool, Realise2, which is available at **www.strengths2020.com**.

If you haven't bought the book already...

Now you've got a dilemma. Have you got what you need from this summary, or is the book worth the purchase price?

Go on, buy it. You won't regret it. Buy two even – one for your boss.

Remember, successful people read more books than unsuccessful people.

This is certainly a book that will help you be more successful.

Contents

Series Editor's Foreword

The publication of *The Strengths Book* marks another significant milestone in the CAPP Press *Strengthening the World* series. As will be familiar to readers of *Average to A+* will be familiar, a key requirement for the strengths approach is a shared language of strengths. This shared language will allow people to be talking about the same things, in the same terms, and in the same language, when they are talking about strengths — rather than misunderstanding each other and being bedevilled by a lack of clarity because there isn't a shared strengths terminology. Over the last few years, this need has started to be addressed, and the sixty strengths of Realise2 that are included here in *The Strengths Book* are another major step in this direction.

Further, the evidence continues to build for the benefits that come through using strengths, as this volume and the scientific source materials testify.

There is also a notable and significant developmental trend through the titles included in the CAPP Press *Strengthening the World* series. *Average to A+* set out the theoretical and empirical underpinnings of the strengths approach. *Celebrating Strengths: Building Strengths-based Schools* focused specifically on the applications of strengths in school settings.

Now, *The Strengths Book* introduces the Realise2 model of strengths assessment and development, as well as featuring five case studies of applications of Realise2 in different settings, together with a detailed exploration of each of the sixty strengths included in Realise2 — their strengths symbol, their definition, identification, catchphrase, Hall of Fame exemplars, leisure suggestions, career guidance, relationship tips — and even cautionary notes about what to watch out for so that they don't become overplayed.

This book is a truly rich strengths resource that will speak to readers who want to identify and develop their own strengths, build their confidence, be more successful, enjoy better relationships, or improve their skills and strategies as parents, as managers and leaders of people, or simply as fulfilled and fully-functioning human beings.

In sum, I am deeply proud to introduce to you *The Strengths Book*, another worthy addition to the CAPP Press *Strengthening the World* series. These books are part of our continued efforts to build a library of strengths knowledge, resources, and applications, the focus of which is to enable and support people and organisations in using their strengths to strengthen others. Together, we are making a difference.

Alex Linley
Series Editor, CAPP Press, *Strengthening the World* series

Preface

This book represents the product of thousands of hours of collective effort and experience in our work on strengths. We have read extensively to understand more about strengths. We have watched and listened for strengths in people in our daily interactions. We have explored how to identify, classify and measure strengths. We have advised organisations on how to manage people for their strengths, and how to best develop people through building on their strengths. We have conducted the research that provides some of the scientific underpinnings for the benefits of the strengths approach. We do this, above all, because we know that realising strengths makes a difference. This book will show you how, and how you can harness the benefits of the strengths approach for yourself.

The book is in three parts. In Part One, we introduce you to five case studies that illustrate the benefits of realising strengths in different settings and life contexts. We also provide an overview of the evidence for the benefits of strengths use, together with providing ten top tips for strengthspotting.

In Part Two, we examine the Realise2 model for the assessment and development of strengths. Realise2 assesses strengths according to the three dimensions of energy, performance, and use, which are then combined to determine whether something is a realised strength, an unrealised strength, a learned behaviour, or a weakness. When you know this, we then tell you what to do with them — whether it is to marshal realised strengths, to maximise unrealised strengths, to moderate learned behaviours, or to minimise weaknesses. And we show you how.

In Part Three, we explore the sixty strengths that are included in Realise2 - their strengths symbol, their definition, identification, catchphrase, Hall of Fame exemplars, leisure suggestions, career guidance, relationship tips — and even cautionary notes about what to watch out for so that the strength doesn't become overplayed. Our intent in doing so is to deepen your understanding of each of these sixty strengths, but specifically to support you in knowing more about those which matter most to you.

Working on this book has been a transformative experience for all of us. We hope that in doing so, we have been able to help you in transforming yourself — through building on your strengths and realising the best of you.

Alex Linley, Janet Willars, Robert Biswas-Diener
Coventry, UK
February 2010

Part One
Case Studies in Strengthening

Simon Lester:
Becoming a Better People Manager

Simon Lester's life is pretty good, even really good sometimes, but never great. In his early forties, he's married with two children and a mortgage to pay, which he does working as a production department manager in a large car component manufacturing company. Simon did quite well at school — especially on the football field, where he played centre half for both school and district. He didn't go to university but instead started his career as an apprentice. Why he ended up in manufacturing, he didn't really know — except perhaps that that was where his dad had worked, and there had been an opportunity close to home when he was leaving school. It was probably a result of the old adage "right time, right place, right face."

If you watch him carefully when he walks, you can detect a slight stiffness in his left leg — the result of an old knee injury from his footballing days. He's gained a few pounds since then — "Haven't we all?!" would be his defence — but at a little over six feet tall he carries it well. His hair matches the colour of the wall panels in his office, a sort of powdery blonde. Its styling seems to reflect the presentation of his desk — a slight look of disorder and disarray, but that nonetheless leaves you with the reassurance that he is pretty much in command of what's happening.

Simon has worked hard and progressed well over the last twenty-five years. So much so, that he has recently been promoted, and now has a team of 80 people in the department he manages, with ten supervisors reporting in to him directly.

Simon thinks of himself as a process person rather than a people person, something probably ingrained through his PRINCE2 project management training, which emphasised plan and process, and seemed to forget people altogether. Notwithstanding this, Simon has always seemed to do well enough with the people side of what he needs to do. His 360-degree feedback scores are strong for process and project management, and okay but not glowing for motivating and managing his people. His financial, commercial and strategic alignment scores are all pretty solid too.

In rare quiet moments, maybe on a Friday evening before he leaves for the weekend, or in the occasional respite from the hustle and bustle of everyday management life, he thinks about the other managers elsewhere in the plant, wondering what it is that they do differently to him. The best managers, he reckons, seem to be so much more natural in how they deal with their people. But that has never really been his bag.

Even so, he has to admit that it's not all bad. His people generally do a good job for him, so on the one hand he thinks he hasn't got too much to complain about. On the other hand, there's still that niggling sense that he could do better, that he's just missing... *something*. Not a sense that had usually bothered him enough to do anything more about it, but just a niggle cropping up now and again.

On the surface, and to most people's eyes, things look pretty good for Simon. He even tries to convince you of that himself. At least, that is, until he builds a trust with you and starts to open up a bit more. And when he does, then you start to see that while things are maybe just about okay with him, they are not actually as rosy as they otherwise seemed.

Leaning back in his faux-leather office chair, his desk strewn with project management print-outs, spine-bound briefing reports, and a half-eaten chicken tikka sandwich, Simon starts to open up about what isn't quite right. Being honest, he admits he is feeling increasingly short-tempered and under pressure in his life. His recent promotion has ramped up the pressure, and he's actually questioning whether he is up to his new role.

His wife and daughter complain that he doesn't spend enough time with them, always working late in the week and then engrossed in his newspaper or watching the sport on TV at the weekends — "With the hours I work, I need time to relax," Simon defends himself. His son, Jake, is the apple of his eye — playing football for the local under-12s as a centre half, just like Simon did in his day.

This, it turns out, is where Simon's passion comes to life: he loves to watch Jake play football, and has a keen eye for the game — so much so that for the last couple of years he has taken over coaching the under-12s side. He is there pretty much every weekend, running up and down as he shouts from the touchline about how they should be aware of each other's positional play, what to watch out for, who is best placed to do what. He sees instinctively what each boy can do well and how they can best contribute to the team. When half-times come, he marshals the boys around him, giving them each individual feedback, before summing up with what they need to do collectively to perform as a team.

* * * *

I'm sat talking with Simon because things have happened lately that really got him thinking. First, he feels like he is starting to crack under the pressure of the job. The car market has taken a nosedive, and there is relentless scrutiny from above on cutting costs and operational efficiencies. As well as this, people are worried about the future of the plant: the threat of redundancies lurks around the corner if things don't turn around for them. Second, as the new boy in post, he feels like he's on trial — and that he's not necessarily making the grade. "A step too far for you, Lester?" one of his peers, Paul Savage, had taunted him in the gents. Of course, Paul had missed out on the promotion himself, so it could have been sour grapes. Still, it hit a nerve in Simon that was a bit too close to home.

Looking around his office, you get a sense of the things he has tried. The partition walls are broken up by ubiquitous inspirational management posters — "There's no I in team," "Success: The surest way not to fail is to determine to succeed" and "Respect: Give it to get it." The dried-out Boston fern sits on the window sill supporting well-thumbed copies of *Who Moved my Cheese?*, *The Seven Habits of Highly Effective People*, and *The One-Minute Manager*. In the corner, nestling on top of his bookcase, are the dusty black ring-binders that evidence his attendance at various management training courses over the years.

Simon's teams at work have usually done okay, but he is frustrated by the fact that he doesn't quite have the ability to understand and motivate them like other managers seem to be able to do — especially the managers he reads about in the management books.

The final thing, it turns out, is pretty critical for Simon: his latest 360-degree feedback scores put him on amber in the company's traffic light grading system. Amber means that he'll get the support to turn things around, but that ultimately it's up to him. "Going back to my footballing days," he explains, "This would be like getting a yellow card. Only this time it's much more serious."

If you're a manager yourself, or anything like a veteran of management training courses similar to those that Simon had clocked up, the chances are you'll know exactly the sense of confused frustration that hung in the air of his office that day.

* * * *

Simon Lester could be any one of any number of managers we have met and worked with over the years. Recently promoted on the basis of his technical ability and professional expertise, he is starting to grapple with the fact that moving up the managerial ladder almost always requires people management responsibilities. It's as if organisations have been deliberately designed to make it difficult for managers — especially managers from a technical background or speciality who don't naturally lean towards the people side of things. As Simon put it himself, "Spreadsheets and project management plans always do what you tell them to do, and you know what you're going to get out of the other end. With people, that's almost never the case."

And therein lays the crux of Simon's problem: he has been trained to think in terms of plans, processes, and project management. He deals with numbers, with projections, with machinery throughput and production output, all of which can be carefully calibrated, measured, and controlled. But you can't do that to people: they don't like it. People want to be autonomous, responsible for themselves and their output, to feel a sense of progress in what they are doing; they want to contribute, to make a difference, and to feel valued and appreciated for doing so. It sounds obvious, but common sense does not always mean common practice: people are a different breed to spreadsheets and project management plans, and they need to be treated differently.

Simon's Realise2 report paints a clear picture. With realised strengths in Pride, Personal Responsibility, Improver, Persistence, Explainer, Resolver and Action, it's clear that he someone who is strongly focused on getting things done and doing them well. His learned behaviours are Planful, Detail, Adherence and Time Optimiser, which give a good insight into what he has picked up over the years in his job and what he has been rewarded for — which is no surprise really, given his project management background and training. They also suggest some of the reasons why he may now be feeling the pressure, because over time, if learned behaviours are over-used, it can lead to disengagement and burn-out. Simon wasn't quite there yet, but the early signs were not encouraging, and indicated that was the path he was headed down if he didn't change things.

Simon's unrealised strengths suggested some of the characteristics on which he might be able to draw in making the changes he needs to make: Incubator, Enabler, Feedback, Judgement, Strategic Awareness, Innovation and Equality. His weaknesses didn't appear to be impacting too much on his current situation: Scribe, Narrator and Connector.

Looking at Simon's Realise2 profile overall, we agreed that it was more the case that over time he had become the job, allowing himself to be defined by what his work expected of him, rather than shaping his work to fit better with what he naturally brought to it. This is something that is always a challenge in large organisations, and especially those organisations that are process- and plan-oriented, because any deviance from the established norm is considered to be "error" — as a result, it is guarded against and rejected if it ever happens. Conformity and compliance can rule; creativity can be squeezed out.

So, what to do about it? Simon's presenting challenge was that he recognised he needed to be better at managing his people, and yet he felt that he was actually getting worse. The hours, the relentless focus on sticking to protocol, delivering on time with the minimum of error (3.4 defects in 1,000,000 parts was the new target, driven by the company's application of Six Sigma manufacturing processes), while always meeting budget — all this was ultimately taking its toll. Simon was spending more and more of his time doing things that drained him, but that nonetheless he could do well — and because he did them well, his bosses expected more of him, rewarded and promoted him as a result, not recognising the emotional impact it was having — because they were never around to see it. For Simon, the combination of Pride and Personal Responsibility ran through him deeply. As a result, he strove constantly to ensure that he did his best, delivering a top quality job and never letting anyone down.

But the way in for things to change was through harnessing his realised strengths of Resolver and Improver. Simon recognised he had a problem, he wanted to fix it, and he wanted to get better at it. Combined with this, Simon has a light bulb moment when he makes the connection between what he does every weekend on the under-12s football pitch, and how he can translate that into what he needs to do at work.

Enabler and Feedback were unrealised strengths for him — at least at work — but he used them every weekend with the under-12s. Seeing this connection, Simon recognises how he has put an artificial wall between who he is at play and who he is at work. At work, the unceasing project focus has started to grind him down; at play, he recharges by coaching and developing others (albeit 10- and 11-year old footballers). Recognising this, he starts to focus on how he can take what he does with the football team and apply it to his work teams — give individualised feedback in real time, set collective goals, identify what each person does best and in which role they can best perform — what we would call strengthspotting.

We also note the interaction between Action as a realised strength and Incubator as an unrealised strength. Incubator — having time to think — was always being squeezed out by the focus on getting things done, which played very well into Simon's Action strength — getting stuck in and making things happen. Because of this, Simon was losing sight of the bigger picture and not always making the right calls on what he needed to do.

Together, we developed a way forward that would allow Simon to draw on the best of himself as a way of meeting and overcoming the challenges he was increasingly facing as a people manager. We blocked the time of his daily 40-minute drive to and from work, so instead of this time being filled with catch-up calls and voicemail messages, Simon actually had the time to step back and incubate on the things he needed to think about in order to make better decisions.

Yet, the real step forward was Simon's connecting of his under-12s football team coaching with how he manages his team at work. Joining the dots of his own ability, Simon recognised that, with a few adjustments, he did know what he needed to do to manage, coach, encourage and develop his people in his new role. And he set to work on doing so with gusto.

* * * *

The next performance review season is coming around, and so we meet again to check on Simon's progress. "We've just all gone through giving our 360 ratings again," he shares. "We haven't got the results back yet — they're due in a couple of weeks — but actually, I'm no longer worried about this like I was before. I know, just from how I am working with my people and how they are working with me, that things are better. I often catch myself thinking, 'How would I handle this with the under-12s?' And then it seems much easier. I still use my drive to and from work to incubate, as you called it, and that has really helped. I can't say that I do it every time — the pressure of the job means that you have to be almost constantly available — but at least this doesn't take all of my time, as it did before."

"I recognise I'll probably never be the best people manager the company has ever seen, but I can certainly do a good enough job in the way that is right for me. And that has been the real realisation — the light-bulb moment — that you don't have to manage people according to some formula that is prescribed in a management text book, but that you can — and should — do it in the way that's right for you and right for them."

* * * *

As Simon Lester's example illustrates, none of us are equipped with what it takes to be brilliant at everything. The myth of the well-rounded individual that is sought by competency frameworks is just that — an utter myth. Instead, the secret to success lies in making the best of what we have and aligning it effectively to what we want to achieve. It is only in doing so that we are able to achieve genuine success and realise the best of ourselves.

*   *   *   *

Simon Lester found that he was able to improve his people management skills — and his relationship with his wife — by strengthspotting, or noticing what it is that people do well and love to do. You can assess your own strengthspotting abilities by completing the Strengthspotting Scale below. There is also a downloadable version available at **www.strengths2020.com**, together with Alex Linley's Top Ten Strengthspotting Tips, which are included later in this first part of the book.

THE STRENGTHSPOTTING SCALE

The items below ask you about identifying what other people do well. Please respond to each item honestly, using the scale below, to indicate how much you agree or disagree with that statement. There are no right or wrong answers.

1	2	3	4	5	6	7
Strongly disagree	Disagree	Slightly disagree	Neither agree or disagree	Slightly agree	Agree	Strongly agree

1. I am able to identify people's strengths with ease ____

2. I get a real buzz from identifying strengths in people ____

3. I notice people's strengths all the time ____

4. I believe I should be on the lookout for other people's strengths ____

5. In the past month I have suggested to a friend or colleague to try out their strengths on a new task ____

6. I am very effective at spotting strengths in people ____

7. It makes me feel good when I notice a strength in someone ____

8. No matter where I am or what I am doing, I find that I am spotting strengths in people ____

9. It is very important to pay attention to people's strengths and what they do well _____

10. I give people suggestions for strengths use and development frequently _____

11. I find it easy to identify people's strengths _____

12. I get a deep sense of fulfilment from helping people to see what their strengths are _____

13. I find myself telling people about their strengths all the time _____

14. I believe I have a responsibility to identify and develop strengths in others _____

15. I always seem to know who would be the best person for which job and why _____

16. I am skilled at spotting people's strengths _____

17. Spotting strengths in people makes me feel happy _____

18. I find myself identifying strengths in people in a wide variety of situations _____

19. Helping people to understand their strengths is deeply important to me _____

20. People appreciate my strengths insights because my insights help them to do their best work _____

How to score: Add up your responses for items 1, 6, 11 and 16 for Strengthspotting − Ability (how good you are at Strengthspotting). Add up your responses for items 2, 7, 12, and 17 for Strengthspotting − Emotional (how much of an emotional buzz you get from Strengthspotting). Add up your responses for items 3, 8, 13, and 18 for Strengthspotting − Frequency (how often you get to practice your Strengthspotting). Add up your responses for items 4, 9, 14, and 19 for Strengthspotting − Motivation (how motivated you are to be a strengthspotter). Add up your responses for items 5, 10, 15, and 20 for Strengthspotting — Application (how effective you are in applying your Strengthspotting to make a difference). Higher scores across all of the dimensions indicate people who are naturally better strengthspotters.

Jane Turner:
Discovering Herself and Making a Difference

Approaching her 40s, Jane is at that stage of life where she is starting to question herself and her life. Has she made the right decisions? Has she done the right things? Has she lived life to the full so far? If she were to die tomorrow, would it be without regrets? Even as she says this, you can see the doubt and the guilt etched across her face. Small worry lines crinkle across her forehead and tentative crow's feet seem to break out from the corners of her eyes. In so many ways, Jane seems to carry the burdens of so many of the women of the world, as some historians would argue indeed, as women have done for all time — putting themselves last and everyone and everything else first. Service so often seems to be the woman's preserve, and as Jane will tell you, for many women, it feels as if the world expects it to be ever thus.

Jane married relatively young — at 22 years of age — and feels as if she has dedicated her life to her family. Most likely, this is because she has. After her A-levels she stayed around at home, balancing her job at the Little Stars children's day nursery with helping her mother, who was first fighting and then recovering from breast cancer. Jane's husband, Richard, is the IT Systems Director for a major council in the district next to where they live. Ever since BlackBerrys arrived, she has felt like he was having an affair — only with his BlackBerry, rather than another woman. People come to the IT Director when it isn't working, not when it is — so Richard's life has been lived by jumping from resolving one problem and on to trying to sort out the next. He has done it constantly, always knowing that Jane would be behind him to pick up the pieces and take care of whatever needed to be taken care of at home.

As a result of this, it was always Jane who juggled the domestic priorities. With Richard at work the hours he was, she didn't feel she had any choice. Once the children had been fed, washed and dressed, the school runs navigated, and the house maintained, Jane was then back to pick the boys up again at their end of their day. On the odd weekend and evening, her service continued, because Jane was an active member of the Parent Teacher Association (PTA) at the boys' school, organising fundraisers like the Christmas fayre and summer barbecue. Any time she managed to squeeze for herself in between, she spent with her friends who found themselves caught in the same intransigent loop. "Always Jane, always there for everyone," was what she told herself, and what her family seemed to expect, for that was their implicit contract.

At least, it had been, until now. Jane is increasingly starting to question what she wants, and why she does what she does. Over the last few years, as the children had grown older — two boys, Michael and Sam, aged 15 and 11 years respectively — Jane has worked in a part-time job as a secretarial assistant at the primary school in the village where they lived. It had suited her perfectly: school term time hours of work, being close by for the boys while they attended the school, and when Michael moved up to secondary school, he'd quickly been able to fend for himself.

She remembered the words of the Headmaster on the Open Evening for new entrants — "I understand that you will all feel anxious about your children moving up to secondary school. This might be the first time they have gone to school this far from home, it might be the first time they will have taken the bus on their own, or been responsible for themselves in this way. But believe me, within two weeks, you'll think they have been doing it for years." And he had been right.

Jane had flourished at the school. The children loved her, and she always seemed to be the one who found time to explain things to them when they asked. She hadn't even been fazed like some of the younger teachers when six-year-old Alice Moxley, wearing a red hair band over her strawberry blond hair that framed a face full of freckles, asked her with shining innocence, "Miss Turner, where do babies come from?" Jane had taken a deep breath and delivered the answer she had to her sons when they were about the same age, explaining confidently that they came from inside their Mummy's tummy. Even so, she was nonetheless relieved when the bell rang for the end of lunchtime — because, she suspected, little Alice was just taking the breath that would have allowed her to ask "And how do they get into their Mummy's tummies?" For children of that age, even with great explanations, it was still a tricky subject!

But now, despite remembering the wonderful times that she has had as a mother to her children, Jane is sat wondering what else there could be to life — and feeling guilty for doing so.

"Whichever way you look at it," she says, "I have everything in life that a woman should wish for. I have a happy marriage, two great children, a nice house, and good friends around me — so why is that not enough?"

As she speaks, I see Jane staring at something that seems to be affixed to my forehead, just above my left eye. She focuses intently, fixated on it, and her voice trails off....

"Of course, this is all because I was told I could not do it," is what she eventually whispers.

But it's not Jane's voice speaking, at least not the voice of Jane who is approaching 40: it's the voice of a teenage girl, a girl who wants to be a teacher but doesn't believe enough in herself that she ever could be. And when that soft, nervous voice finally finds enough courage to speak at her fifth year Careers Evening, it's crushed back into its dark corner with a cold and inconsiderate, but not necessarily mal-intentioned, *"But you're not an academic."* "Okay," Jane concedes, and in that moment, feels as if the course of her life has been set for ever.

But the spirit in us never dies, and as buried as Jane's inner voice may have become, she has never lost it. The Whisper had never left her. Always in her ear, ephemeral and mysterious, sliding into consciousness in those quiet moments just before she awoke in the morning, or as she gazed out across the skyline. The sense that maybe, just maybe, if she just allowed herself, if she just believed, then maybe she could do it. Even when others had not believed in her, the Whisper had. And over the years, its power had slowly grown, tiny at first, but, like the shoots of a nascent bud pushing up through the earth, the Whisper pushed up through the layers of doubt and rejection until it found the sunlight and nourishment of a child's laughter, a pupil's spark of pride when they understood, or just the smiles that danced across their faces, and were reflected in her own, when the children addressed her as "Miss Turner".

"I've always wanted to do it," she whispers, "always wanted to be a teacher — and always thought that I could be a great one!" her voice raising with that last statement, the emerging roar of conquest still there, undimmed after all these years.

For years, she has put this to the back of her mind, the haunting taunt of "But you're not an academic" being the parade ground refrain that cuts her ambitions back down to size. Supporting her husband to succeed, being a loving wife and an even better mother, these were the characteristics to which she believed she should aspire — and centuries of social conditioning seemed to confirm it: that her place was to serve others, to put herself second, just as her mother had done before her.

Yet, as Jane had settled in to her work at the school, she had increasingly begun to question this. This questioning is a function of at least two things, she thinks:

"As the boys have grown up, they don't need me as much anymore. So whereas I used to pride myself on always being available for them whenever they needed me, if I did that now, I'd spend hours just waiting around for nothing — and they'd have license to treat me as a doormat, which can't be right. And as Richard has grown more successful in his role, he has had more support around him at work — so while the hours are longer and the pressures greater, his life largely takes care of itself."

"But what about me? *What* about me? I have so much that I want to do, so much that I can still give," the whisper rasping out through gritted teeth and tears. "The job at the school was a way to answer this emptiness, to try and give something back. But it was just a small step, a step so small that nobody could criticise it, nobody could tell me that I couldn't do it, nobody could tell me that I wasn't good enough."

"And it has all worked out. I love the work and love being with the children. I volunteer for classroom duties whenever I can, covering for Classroom Support Assistants while they're off, or spending an hour reading with children who needed (ELS) Extra Literacy Support — and the teachers really appreciate it. You can see the difference that it makes, and to see a child get what they need to do to be able to put the letters together to form a word, the words together to make a sentence, and the sentences together to tell a story. Well — there's just nothing like it! It's the best feeling in the world!"

As these hours and interactions mount up, as the success stories build, the Whisper grows stronger. "See, you did okay there." "Look, there's another one you've helped." "What about your own children? They didn't turn out too bad, did they?"

* * * *

Many of us may recognise Jane as the archetypal mother of modern times, caught between the rock of wanting to do the right thing by her children and family, and the hard place of the sacrifices that this service always seems to entail, with her own wants and needs being swallowed up in the guilt in between.

The good news for Jane, however, is that when she understands her Realise2 profile, it helps her to resolve this apparent conundrum. Service, Mission, Enabler, Explainer, Esteem Builder are some of her Realised Strengths, while Narrator, Creativity and Courage are unrealised. Efficacy and Self-awareness are Weaknesses, which might go some way to explaining her own doubts about her abilities —

paradoxical really, when you consider her unwavering belief in the abilities of others.

The key that unlocked this for Jane was realising that who she was and what she had done with her life were inextricably intertwined with what she *wanted* to do with her life. When she looked at her strengths and understood them, she could see why. Service, Mission, Enabler, Explainer, Esteem Builder — these were not the strengths of someone who was necessarily out front at the expense of others. In contrast, just like Jane, if you were to be out front with this strengths profile, it would be being out front to serve, to explain, to enable, to build confidence. And when combined with the potential for developing her unrealised strengths of Narrator and Creativity, it was clear that Jane was the real deal as a teacher. Even if she was still early in her own journey toward realising it, Jane was a natural in doing many of the things, in fact, that great teachers do.

* * * *

Finally, the fateful morning arrives. Jane's BA (Hons) English with ITT application decision letter arrives. She has been accepted! Of all the cards and notes she receives on being accepted for her degree and Initial Teacher Training course, there is one that for her captures it all.

"Bloody well done!" is the inscription, the resolute determination of the celebration mirroring the resolute determination that on many occasions had been the only thing keeping her going. Jane's life wasn't hard by any reasonable standard. What was hard was her maintaining her belief that, yes, even after all this time and after everything, she could do it. Always putting others first, she had lived her life through their eyes, fearing that she was losing sight of who she was or what she wanted.

Now, with her teacher training course acceptance under her belt, Jane is another big step on her way to becoming a teacher in her own right. She knows that this is just the beginning, that there is a lot of hard work to come, yet she is ready for it and fully focused on realising her dream — of being a great teacher.

I firmly believe she will be, whether she is ultimately an "academic" or not.

* * * *

Jane Turner had many things going right in her life, but she wasn't developing herself to make the most of what she had to offer, and as a result she didn't feel as if she was flourishing. You can assess your own flourishing by completing the Flourishing Scale which we have included for you below. There is also a downloadable version available at **www.strengths2020.com**.

THE FLOURISHING SCALE

Below are eight statements with which you may agree or disagree. Using the 1–7 scale below, indicate your agreement with each item by indicating that response for each statement.

1 Strongly disagree	2 Disagree	3 Slightly disagree	4 Neither agree or disagree	5 Slightly agree	6 Agree	7 Strongly agree

1. I lead a purposeful and meaningful life _____

2. My social relationships are supportive and rewarding _____

3. I am engaged and interested in my daily activities _____

4. I actively contribute to the happiness and well-being of others _____

5. I am competent and capable in the activities that are important to me _____

6. I am a good person and live a good life _____

7. I am optimistic about my future _____

8. People respect me _____

How to score: Add the responses, varying from 1 to 7, for all eight items. The possible range of scores is from 8 (lowest possible) to 56 (highest PWB possible). A high score represents a person who is flourishing, with many psychological resources and high well-being.

Source: Diener, E., Wirtz, D., Tov, W., Kim-Prieto, C., Choi. D., Oishi, S., & Biswas-Diener, R. (2009). New measures of well-being: Flourishing and positive and negative feelings. In E. Diener (Ed.) The collected works of Ed Diener (Vol. 3, pp. 247–266). Dordrecht, NL: Springer. Reprinted with permission.

Matt Johnson:
Striving to be a Good Parent

"You never see yourself so clearly as when you are reflected back through the eyes of a child." The words echo around Matt Johnson's head, as they do so often when he hears four-year-old Josh say something back to him and recognises it as a mirror image of himself. In his (very) late twenties, Matt sports a neat brown haircut with slightly tapered sideburns. His eyes are hazel with a bit of a sparkle when they catch the light, sitting aside a slim Greek nose that, as he had found over the years, many women found attractive. Matt has always been recognised as a smart dresser — *Canali* suits and *Segni & Disegni* ties that reflected his love of all sartorial things Italian. At five feet eleven inches, and well-toned with it, he would likely make many women proud to take him home — and their mothers too!

Matt works in professional services for one of the so-called "Big Four" accountancy firms. He had joined them after university (a high 2.1 in History from Bristol) and found the interview process surprisingly easy — it seemed to be more about which university he had gone to and his views on the England cricket team, rather than his aspirations to be an auditor — but so be it, he didn't mind, he had landed the job after all. That was seven years ago, and then Elaine had come along, followed in fairly quick succession by Joshua, their first born. Elaine was three years older than Matt and worked in a solicitor's office in Birmingham. To some, they had married and settled down quickly, but both were grateful to have met the "right" person and so they were happy to get on with it. Between them, they thought that they had figured things out pretty much, and that life was good.

Yet, that wasn't entirely the case for Matt, as became clear when we spoke over coffee after an Emerging Leaders development programme he had attended. Matt is like so many of us who are parents — wanting to do the best he can — *desperately* wanting to do the best he can — but never entirely sure that what he is doing is right. Take his suits, for example. He had always been recognised as the best-dressed in his office. When we meet, however, the stylish cut of his appearance is toned down a little, as has become more of the norm since Josh's arrival — the reason, Matt explains, that he got fed up of his visits to the dry cleaners to deal with the remnants of *Mum's Own Caribbean Casserole with Pork*, or whatever Josh's dish happened to have been that day! As this happened time and again, as well as struggling to reconcile the cost of his suits against the cost of bringing up a baby, he'd started to realise it wasn't worth it. "Practicality over perfection," he tells himself nowadays, and it seems to work.

Josh has just started in the reception year at school. As Matt talks, it's clear that this has presented a new level of challenge for him, even opened up an old seam of anxiety. Matt feels that he has always been the apple of Josh's eye, knowing everything and able to do everything, so that Josh looks up to him as his hero — as every father would want of their son. But lately, Matt confesses, since Josh has started at school, that hasn't been so much the case. Josh is starting to question him now, showing a resentful confusion if Matt's answer doesn't match up with what the seemingly omniscient Miss Tyson has said at school. As a result, Matt's own anxieties and insecurities about being a parent are starting to creep through.

Truth be told, since Josh was born, his existence has always seemed to throw curve balls to Matt, causing him to remember things long buried, to question things that he never would previously have questioned. He remembers his feelings of being utterly overwhelmed as Elaine approached Josh's due date, wondering — quite irrationally — if he would ever be able to go back to work, or if his life would be changed irrevocably by the arrival of this new child into the world. Of course, he knows now, as he looks back, that this is the same for so many new parents. We think our lives are going to change beyond recognition — and in some ways they do, but in other ways we just adapt and carry on. And of course, when you think about it rationally, anything else is ridiculous: people have been having children for thousands of years before us and life, by definition, just carries on.

Matt remembers whispering to Josh in the first few weeks after he was born that he will always look after him, always be there for him, never let him down, as he held him in his arms, wondering if his life was ever going to be the same again. But since then, how many sports days, how many nativity plays, how many of Josh's friends' birthday parties had he missed?

He justifies it all to himself by saying that he works the hours he does to provide for Josh and Elaine — and also to allow them to be prepared for whatever other little "Josh's" may hopefully come along in the future. The hours might be hell, but at least he can see he is progressing and that he is providing for his family along the way. "I go to work so that we can live in a nice house, and have nice things, and go on holiday to nice places," he tells Josh, which all sounds entirely rational until Josh replies, "But I just want to be with you," his eyes expressing the world-less innocence which only children can feel. "But money doesn't grow on trees," Matt defends himself, time and again, questioning deep down whether he really believes this or whether it's a convenient truth that will protect the status quo for now. "Where does it grow then?" is Josh's killer reply, which Matt doubts even the omniscient Miss Tyson would be able to answer.

These inconvenient truths are starting to eat away at Matt, since too often he hears his father's voice coming back to haunt him: "Go and play for a while, I'm busy," "Not now, Matthew," and the one that hits home the hardest, "What do you think pays for this house, your clothes, the food on the table? Me going to work — that's what. One day you'll understand and appreciate it!!" Is history inescapable, Matt asks himself, or can I write my own life as I want it to be?

His father is still around, and they are in touch regularly enough, but Matt won't be nominating him for the Father of the Year Prize any time soon. Growing up, he had always felt he was not quite up to the mark for his dad, that he could never quite get his approval or meet his expectations. His dad meant well, he was sure, but at least as far as Matt was concerned, he probably didn't get the outcomes he intended — or at least that was what Matt hoped for himself, holding on to the view that his father didn't intend to be as distant and conditional as he experienced him to be.

Matt's own upbringing had been mixed. His mother was a gentle, caring woman, but very much subservient to his military-background father, a hard taskmaster who expected a lot but didn't give a lot back in return, particularly when it came to support or affection. He had high standards of what he expected from his children: always use your manners, beds made every day, uniforms neatly folded and homework done before there is any semblance of fun or relaxation — and most especially before the television goes on, school grades at or striving to be top of the class, no dinner and straight to bed if there was a hint of something not being up to par. The list went on. If you did well, the most you could expect was a firm shake of the hand if you were Matt, or a squeeze of the shoulders and a peck on the cheek if you were Matt's younger sister, Lisa. His approval was always hard to gain, remarkably easy to lose. Lisa seemed to have grasped this a lot better than Matt, and managed to give her father what he wanted (or at least give him the impression that he was getting what he wanted), whereas Matt had never quite mastered this art, and so will always left hungry for more approval, encouragement, or even just acceptance.

The hole this left in him is well hidden, but as Josh is growing up, Matt's concern is that it is getting more raw. Too often he catches himself behaving towards Josh as his own father did towards him, and is caught by the fear that history could be repeating itself, when that is the last thing he wants. After the NCT antenatal classes, he'd read a couple of books, *The Contented Little Baby Book*, which seemed to be all the rage, and, via a discreet recommendation from Elaine's mother, *Dr. Benjamin Spock's Baby and Child Care*, but neither of these had given him what he was looking for.

What was he looking for? As it turned out, that becomes the focus of our conversation, whether Matt intended it that way or not:

"Josh came home from school yesterday, and when I got back, he was all excited about being a painter when he grows up. Miss Tyson had told him that his painting reminded her of a painting by a famous artist called Picasso — 'Pizza-So' Josh called him! — and so he was going on and on about how he was going to be a painter."

"It's great if you enjoy it, but painting won't be a good job for you Josh," Matt described how he found himself saying. "You should get a job where you can progress and make some real money so you can provide for yourself and your family, like a lawyer or an accountant, like me or Mummy."

"I'm not a lawyer, honey, and more to the point, Josh should be able to do whatever he wants to do — and we should be encouraging him," Elaine cut in, exasperated. "You've gotten so that you're always like this, pulling him down and making him fit into your idea of what he should be. Just let him be himself — he's five years old, for God's sake!"

"And with that," Matt explained, "I flipped and stormed out. Something inside me just gave way, Elaine really touched a nerve, and I realised I needed to get to grips with it and sort it out."

* * * *

Matt's story is a story that may resonate with so many of us. We are all actors in the play of our lives, and to a greater or lesser extent, the script may not be one we have necessarily been able to write ourselves. Yet, through recognising where his history had left him, and taking responsibility for what he could do for himself and for others going forward, Matt was able to make the changes he wanted to make.

We used Matt's Realise2 profile to help him shape his actions in the way that were right for him, and so more likely to stick and more likely to enable him to be successful. Matt had Pride, Work Ethic,

Competitive, Improver, Adherence, Detail, and Planful as his most prevalent Realised Strengths. Yet he struggled with Josh, we found, because Unconditionality was a Weakness — and a potential overhang from his own upbringing. Drive, Order and Resilience were Learned Behaviours, perhaps reflecting his internalisation of his father's requirements from childhood — and which no doubt had also played out, and helped him to be rewarded, by being successful at work.

In helping Matt to frame his relationship with Josh through a different lens, we looked at which of his strengths could most effectively help him to do so — and which would make the effort most natural and rewarding for him as well. With Work Ethic as a realised strength, the effort he would commit was without question, and as well as being the cause of some of his parenting heartache up to now, Matt's Improver strength gave him the motivation to do better.

Looking at his strengths profile, however, we agreed that the best way to hook his desire to be a better father for Josh was through the combination of Pride and Competitive. Pride, because he wanted to do a top quality job in everything that he did, and being a parent was no exception. And Competitive, not because he was going to be entering himself for the Father of the Year Awards, but because we saw the opportunity of how he could compete with himself to be a better father than he had been before, as well as striving to be a better father than his had been for him. "History doesn't have to repeat itself," Matt concluded.

* * * *

About six months later we meet again, after one of the follow-ups to the Emerging Leaders programme. "How are things, Matt?" I ask.

"Things are good," Matt replies. "Josh is doing great, and Elaine is happy too. There are still the pressures at work, and it's getting worse with the economic climate, but so be it. Things at home are much improved...And whatever has happened at work, do you know the favourite part of every day for me now? Every night — at least when I'm home in time — as we get Josh ready for bed, I lay him across my lap and walk my fingers up his spine while he tells me about his day. And the way he chuckles as I do it, well, that will stay with me forever. Kids aren't young for long enough these days, so you need to hold on to every memory you can."

* * * *

Matt Johnson found that he was able to overcome the insecurities he faced as a parent through getting to know his strengths, and then thinking about how he could apply them to become a better father. If you want to see how well you know your own strengths, complete the Strengths Knowledge Scale which we have included for you below. There is also a downloadable version available at **www.strengths2020.com**.

THE STRENGTHS KNOWLEDGE SCALE

The following questions ask you about your strengths, that is, the things that you are able to do well or do best. Please respond to each statement using the scale below:

1 Strongly disagree	2 Disagree	3 Slightly disagree	4 Neither agree or disagree	5 Slightly agree	6 Agree	7 Strongly agree

1. Other people see the strengths that I have   ____

2. I have to think hard about what my strengths are   ____

3. I know what I do best   ____

4. I am aware of my strengths   ____

5. I know the things I am good at doing   ____

6. I know my strengths well   ____

7. I know the things I do best   ____

8. I know when I am at my best   ____

How to score: Subtract your response to item number two from 8, then add up your responses to each of the items. Higher scores indicate higher levels of strengths knowledge. People who know their strengths better are more likely to be able to use them and to be effective in doing so.

Source: Govindji, R., & Linley, P. A. (2007). Strengths use, self-concordance and well-being: Implications for strengths coaching and coaching psychologists. *International Coaching Psychology Review, 2* (2), 143–153. Reprinted with permission.

Sara Stewart:
Realising the Best of Her Relationships

Sat opposite her, you wouldn't necessarily believe Sara Stewart's dilemma even if she told you. It's not that she comes across as a liar or inauthentic – far from it! It's just that the dilemma she describes seems to be incongruent with what you experience from her as a person. Her pretty elfin features are framed by a short brown crop that loosely follows the contours of her head. There is a trace of a dimple in each cheek when she smiles, and white teeth that would be perfect except for a small chip off her upper right incisor, the result of an accident with a rogue swing when she was 12 years old. Sara is about 5' 6", a bubbling mixture of confidence and playfulness on the outside, but on the inside lurks an unjustified nervous tension when she meets new people or finds herself in a group.

In her late 20s, one might think that Sara would have overcome this by now. And yet, her story – the story that she tells herself about herself – gives some insights into the reasons why not.

"About four years ago I did an MBTI® [a personality type assessment] when I went on a junior manager development programme, and it told me that I was on the 89th percentile for being introverted...I guess I have always been like that. My dad was always the life and soul of any family gathering, so I just left him to get on with it and sat quietly – and happily – in the corner...Now I try and avoid them, but if I have to go to social events or things, I try to tag along with someone who will do the talking and the schmoozing."

"At school I was popular, but I always had a tight circle of just a few friends – Katy, Lisa and Helen. We're all still good friends today. My wider family is not especially close-knit – we're the sort that get together for weddings and funerals, and then make those false promises that 'We must get together soon,' despite the fact we all know in our hearts that it will never really happen. Life just carries on, whether we like it or not. I am an only child, so I don't really know what it's like to have a brother or sister that I could turn to or confide in."

By any yardstick, Sara is doing pretty well for herself – and for others. Her parents are proud of her – although she still often regresses to the role of the quiet, meek girl in the corner when she occasionally goes to see them. She is successful at work, promoted a couple of times already since she started with the company — a major retail chain specialising in health and beauty — and now she is being prepared for the next step up. To all external appearances, everything would seem to be great for her.

But that is where the niggle comes in. Sara started off as a sales assistant on the cosmetics counter. She took pride in really understanding how the products were made and the quality of their ingredients. She knew her ceramides from her plant extracts, and this always enabled her to have something to talk about with the customers who came in, so the shyness she always felt inside she managed to never let become an issue on the outside. She did well, always managing to hit her monthly sales targets through sharing her knowledge with customers, people enjoyed buying from her. A couple of years in, she became a Cosmetics Counter Supervisor, looking after the small team of three that ran the counter. "But that worked okay too," she tells me, "Because I knew the people and they knew me, and we all got on really well, so it was never an issue."

The next step up was a bit of a bigger jump, to Deputy Store Manager, but again, Sara's experience within the store, and her popularity there, helped her pull it off. She was popular with (most of) her colleagues, and with many of the customers, relationships built up over the seven years that she had been there. This meant that she was effective in taking on the challenges that came her way in the new role, enjoying the stretch and responsibility as she did so.

Now approaching 30, and single, she feels that she is at a crossroads in her life. Her biggest concern is that whatever decision she takes is likely to have consequences that might reverberate for years to come. Sara's dilemma is that she has been told she could be put forward for a stretch promotion to Regional Manager, overseeing the activities and performance of a dozen or so stores within her region.

On the one hand, to be considered is a great honour and a great opportunity. On the other, to be considered fills her with dread, because it will mean that she has to move away from everything that she knows and holds dear in her current role. Worse, she will have to take on a very different set of responsibilities and challenges — responsibilities and challenges which, being honest with herself as she always is, she questions whether she is capable of living up to.

We talk about how she has overcome challenges before, since each of her promotions has, by definition, been a step up from where she was previously. As Sara talks, I see fleeting glimpses of the nervousness that she showed when we first met: the self-doubt, the critical self-talk inside her head, the whispers of anxiety and insecurity, all of which serve to undermine the confidence which, by any other metric, should be there in abundance.

Sara's biggest challenge, simply put, is people. More specifically, it is meeting and getting to know new people. She has always been happy with her close circle of friends, but struggles outside of them when she doesn't have a framework — like the sales patter of the cosmetics counter — to help her feel safe. As she herself recognises, this could be one of the reasons why she hasn't yet found that special someone with whom to share her life. Her last long-term relationship came to an end a couple of years ago, and she admits that since then she has struggled to let people get close to her, being too wary of getting hurt if they did.

At work, at least until now, she has managed to put on a mask of sociability for long enough to get to know people. From there it becomes easier, because once she knows them, she is very good at building relationships with them that will stand the test of time. Yet her challenge is stepping over that boundary in the first place, the move from "don't know" to "making contact with."

Over the years, she tells me, she has read a few books on the topic, things like *The Art of Connecting, The Fine Art of Small Talk*, and *Networking Like a Pro!* Her problem is that the approaches they recommend always seem to her to be false and inauthentic, even mechanical. "I always feel like those sort of books require me to sell my soul," she explains over a small macchiato, "or that I have to play a game, or act a part, in order to build a rapport with someone. But that just doesn't work for me — it's not how I work, and I don't want relationships that feel false from the beginning."

If Sara took the Regional Manager job, it would require her to stretch herself like she had never stretched before. If she didn't, it had the potential to be a career-progress-ending move. Like so many other organisations, her organisation had the usual up-or-out progress culture. This can be typical where senior managers haven't yet recognised that sometimes the best place for people could be at the level they are already operating, playing to their strengths.

Equally as challenging, Sara was grappling with the fundamental identity question of whether she would be selling herself out, and double-crossing her nature, by switching to become what she perceived was needed. She had read in one of her favourite books, *Self-promotion for Introverts*, that society was inherently geared towards the visibility of extroverts. Even so, introverts have many strengths that help them succeed and complement the strengths and needs of their extrovert cousins. This is an approach that resonates with her, and it forms the basis for our subsequent conversations: looking at how Sara could enjoy better relationships by building on her strengths and making the most of the talents she has within her already.

* * * *

Sara is an example of the classic case of an introvert living in an extroverted world. Society tends to reward us for being extroverts: just look at the whole celebrity culture and how people are rewarded for putting themselves on display. Yet there's about half the population that aren't naturally like this, and can find themselves having to learn how to cope and fit in with what society expects, indeed requires, of them (note to the reader: I, AL, am one). But rather than having to "sell our souls" as Sara is concerned about, there are numerous ways in which we can draw from our strengths to achieve the outcomes we want. Sara's example illustrates the ways she found to do this.

Her Realise2 report shows realised strengths in Relationship Deepener, Authenticity, Esteem Builder, Courage, Humility, and Optimism. Sara is great at building relationships that will stand the test of time, as she has done with the people with whom she works. She is deeply true to herself and prepared to stand up for what she believes in, which is why she struggles with feeling false or inauthentic. She can help others to feel good about themselves and has a generally positive outlook on life. Yet she's also very likely to "hide her light under a bushel", which, combined with her introverted nature, means that she's unlikely to be the person standing out front — unless something really matters to her, in which case she will take the risks she believes in.

Sara's unrealised strengths are Emotional Awareness, Empathic Connection, and Equality. Her learned behaviours show up as Competition, Planful, and Persuasion — things she has learned to do through being successful in her role. Tellingly, her weaknesses come through as Rapport Builder and Centred. In combination, this could well explain why she feels nervous in new situations and with new people.

Taking her Realise2 report as our guide, we look at how she can use her strengths to overcome her weaknesses. Her big challenge is in meeting new people and building rapport in the short term, combined with a lack of confidence that leaves her feeling anxious. And yet, she has unrealised strengths that help her to sense how others are feeling

(Emotional Awareness) and connect with them at an emotional level (Empathic Connection). These are the strengths that also serve her in building deep relationships with people, but her anxiety has given her a mental block when it comes to using these with people she meets for the first time. She strives to treat people equally (Equality) and she can help them to feel good about themselves (Esteem Builder), so we use these in combination to help her improve in getting to know people for the first time.

The first thing that comes up is a fundamental mindset shift: Sara discloses how she has had an almost visceral reaction just to the title of *Networking Like a Pro*, which "makes me feel like I have to sell myself in order to be successful."

Sara starts to try it out and finds that, actually, she can do this extroversion thing pretty well — even enjoying the paradox of knowing who she is and being very comfortable with it, but at the same time being able to flex her style and behave differently, still in a way that is right for her. Like a snake that has shed its skin through growing a new one, sloughing off the old identity because it has been outgrown and is no longer useful, Sara is now a different person, in some ways, but in others she is just the same, always herself, but better.

She starts to recognise that her relationships with people don't need to be as analogue as an on/off switch, she either has a relationship with somebody or she doesn't. Instead, she comes to recognise that, like many things in life, the amount one invests in relationships can be likened to a volume control, you can turn it up or turn it down, but it never has to be fully on or indeed fully off.

Letting go of the life narrative that had started to constrict her, Sara embraces the fact that she can become who and what she wants to be without letting go of who, at her core, she already is. She can get bigger than the situations she faces, she doesn't need to change herself beyond recognition in order to fit into them.

*   *   *   *

Just over four months after she has started in the new Regional Manager role, we meet again.

"So, Sara, you've had your proverbial first 90 days in the new role. How's it going?"

"Like any new job, it's had its fair share of ups and downs, but not in the ways that I would have expected. I feel that I am getting better and better at making connections with people and getting to know them. Funnily enough, the bit I'm struggling with the most is finding my way to the different stores I need to visit — even with the Garmin satnav that I bought myself as a well done for getting the promotion!"

"I'm meeting new people every week, and as soon as I do, instead of getting nervous, I focus my attention on how they are feeling and use this as my way to connect with them. It's working really well! My senior manager has told me that people have given him lots of positive feedback about me, and he's very pleased with the impact that I am having already, which has to be good news..."

"...but the even better news is that maybe, just maybe, I've met someone. It's still early days, but I'm enjoying myself and having fun. We'll see how it goes!"

This is what we see so often through the results of our strengths work: that people can be transformed both professionally *and* personally through letting go of their self-stories about who they are not, and instead realising the best of who they are.

* * * *

The biggest issue that Sara Stewart grappled with was how to be herself at the same time as fitting in with other people. Her personal authenticity was at the heart of this challenge. If you want to assess your own authenticity, complete the Authenticity Scale that we have included for you below. There is also a downloadable version available at **www.strengths2020.com**.

THE AUTHENTICITY SCALE

The following items ask about you. After deciding whether an item describes you very well, or does not describe you at all, please use the 7-point scale to respond to that item. For example, if an item describes you very well, please enter "7". If an item does not describe you at all, please enter "1". If you decide that an item is in between, please enter the number that describes you best. There are no right or wrong answers. Please give the answer that best describes you.

1 Does not describe me at all	2	3	4	5	6	7 Describes me very well

1. I think it is better to be yourself than to be popular.   ____

2. I don't know how I really feel inside.   ____

3. I am strongly influenced by the opinions of others. _____

4. I usually do what other people tell me to do. _____

5. I always feel I need to do what others expect me to do. _____

6. Other people influence me greatly. _____

7. I feel as if I don't know myself very well. _____

8. I always stand by what I believe in. _____

9. I am true to myself in most situations. _____

10. I feel out of touch with the "real me". _____

11. I live in accordance with my values and beliefs. _____

12. I feel alienated from myself. _____

How to score:
Add up your responses to items 1, 8, 9 and 11 to give a score for Authentic Living (how much you feel you are being authentic in how you live your life). Add up your responses to items 3, 4, 5 and 6 to give a score for Accepting External Influence (how much you are influenced by other people). Add up your responses to items 2, 7, 10 and 12 to give a score for Self-Alienation (how much you feel alienated or out of touch with yourself). Higher scores reflect higher levels of each dimension.

Source: Copyright © 2008 by the American Psychological Association. Reproduced with permission. The official citation that should be used in referencing this material is: Wood, A. M., Linley, P. A., Maltby, J., Baliousis, M., & Joseph, S. (2008). The authentic personality: A theoretical and empirical conceptualization, and the development of the Authenticity Scale. *Journal of Counseling Psychology*, 55, 385–399. No further reproduction or distribution is permitted without written permission from the American Psychological Association.

Ashok Shah:
Finding a More Rewarding Career after Redundancy

Ashok Shah is a proud man. You can see his pride in his countenance and bearing, the quality stamp of a job well done running throughout everything he does. Even now, approaching his mid-fifties, his back is ramrod straight, his frame slim. His shoulders are broad inside a smart, black, single-breasted blazer with gold buttons that sets off his look as if he were the ship's purser on an expensive ocean-going liner. Who knows, in another life he may have been. He wears steel-rimmed glasses of squared-off ovals, sitting precisely on each ear, nestled in the tufts of greyish-white hair that seem to sprout from either side of his head, giving him the look of a wise old owl.

Ashok has always taken pride in who he is and what he does, having "bootstrapped myself up," as he likes to put it, telling the story of how his parents set out on the Great Journey from their remote village home in Gujarat. Leaving a home that was built of little more than old wooden railcar boards and faded blue plastic sheeting worked into the splinter breaks, "They barely had two rupees to rub together when they set out," Ashok explains, "and even then, they bore the portrait of the Monarch of Great Britain. I remember my father telling me the story of how England was home to the best banks in the world, and so that is why he came here — to try and make his way in the world."

Slowly and surely work and resolve of Ashok's mother and father had paid off, and the ethic had been passed down to their son. Ashok and his wife now own the pleasant three-bed semi-detached house in which they live on a comfortably middle-class, urban residential estate. The mortgage is paid off and their two children, a son and a daughter, have both grown up and gone on successfully making their own way in the world.

"My greatest achievements," Ashok says, as he talks about his children, flushing with pride, his back even straighter than it was before, as he fills out with emotion at the thought of his children and what his efforts, in turn, have enabled them to do.

Yet, as becomes apparent as we talk, Ashok's pride in his children provides only one part of his life's meaning. The other has always been his job — working in a bank. "People said about me that if you cut me through, I'd bleed our corporate colours," Ashok explained, "I lived and breathed the bank. I was so grateful for the job and the opportunity, so determined to pay them back and never let them down."

Now, though, Ashok feels as though he has been slapped in the face before being kicked out of the door by the seat of his pants. He is to become another casualty of the Great Recession of 2008–2009, another faceless statistic that conceals the reality of a life in turmoil, relational networks uprooted, social standing turned on its head.

Ashok is the classic employee who for years has kept his head down and done what's needed, keeping the boss happy and making the bank money; money which in turn has paid his salary at the end of every month and enabled him to provide for his family. Ashok has seen headcount reductions before that variously went by the euphemisms of downsizing, rightsizing, restructuring, or workforce reconfiguration. "In quieter moments," he confides in me, "I play with what words they could come up with for this next – *human capital reduction, company-employee need matching,* even *wrongsizing* – who knows!"

And yet Ashok was grateful that it was never him. He had held his breath many times before when redundancies came around, but thankfully his work ethic and commitment seemed to have paid off, and over time he had allowed himself to feel – just occasionally – that he had maybe done enough to earn his right to stay. He had seen the sacrificial slaughter of older (and more experienced!) workers at the Cult of Youth every time a "restructuring" came round, but he always chose to see it through the eyes of those younger employees who were promoted and moved on and up, just as had happened to him over the years. Only this time, he wasn't the younger employee getting promoted and moving on and up. His role as a Senior Wealth Manager was disappearing. He was the older, experienced hand who was being moved out...

But he had been through worse before, and he could do it again. Hadn't Hanuman brought back the whole mountain when he couldn't find the sanjivani herb that Lakshmana needed? Ashok would need to uphold the same great strength and determination to find another way through this transition. He was determined to find this within himself, and to live up to the trials, tribulations and sacrifices of his ancestors that allowed him to be where he was today.

It was this resolve that had brought Ashok onto one of the outplacement programmes offered by his company. As part of the programme, as well as looking at the usual things on change curves and the change process, Ashok had been helped to get things into a different perspective. He had learned about so-called "affective forecasting", which he basically understood to mean that we were even worse at predicting our emotional reactions to future events than we were at predicting the weather, as well as about some of the more creative and effective ways in which people went about finding new jobs, such as the "doing a life-changing job hunt" exercise that was described in *What Colour is Your Parachute?*

Ashok had also been able to spend some time looking at his strengths, and distinguishing them from what he now knew to be his *learned behaviours*, as well as understanding more about his weaknesses. This was the part of the workshop that had really captured the attention of the group, and Ashok was no exception.

As Ashok had worked through the exercises and discussions to deepen his understanding of what he loves to do and does well (his strengths), contrasting them with what he can do well but doesn't enjoy (his learned behaviours), and what he does but is actually bad at doing and is de-energised by (his weaknesses), a whole new vista of self-understanding opened up for him.

Ashok came to realise that he had become a manager because that was the natural next step at that point in time: a promotion with more money, more responsibility, and more prospects, together with a black leather chair rather than one of those dusty brown call centre-style swivel ones with the black levers that never quite seemed to work properly.

For the last twenty-two years, that is what Ashok had been — a manager of others. The titles of his position changed from time to time, the jurisdiction and remit changed, but he was always a manager: holding people accountable, setting priorities, managing tasks and managing people to get the job done. The pats on the back had served as effective carrots over the years, and the stick was always there discreetly behind the scenes. If you didn't do what was needed, then you could be heading out of the door, with all the ignominy that involved.

Yet, as his son and daughter had grown older, Ashok had found himself thinking increasingly about the example he was setting them: "On quiet moments as I drove to work, I would often find myself thinking about whether it was enough to work to live and nothing more, or whether there was, indeed, something more than this," he disclosed. "But more than anything, I questioned the example that I was setting for my children as they grew up, influenced undoubtedly by the example that my own parents had set for me. They had inspired me with high expectations. Was I really living up to the expectations they had created in me?"

Now faced with the reality of not working at the bank anymore, Ashok finds his anxiety about his identity even more pronounced. The creeping dread of whether he would ever work again; the denial that there was a problem; the anger and resentment at everything he had given to the bank over the last twenty-eight years and beyond. Yes, there was the pay-off, of course, and that took the edge off things for him financially, but it did nothing to assuage the assault on the meaning of his existence and his sense of self-worth, both of which had been defined in substantial part through his job with the bank.

He had seen people move out into early retirement before, with so many promises that they would reduce their golf handicap, master a foreign language, or write the novel that had been sitting within them all their lives. But, almost always and almost inevitably, none of this ever came to pass. Instead, they slipped into longer lie-ins and lunches, whiling away the time until the next live football on TV, looking at the guy next door with his part-time van driving job and thinking "I'd love a job like that!" How their aspirations had shrunken. The tragedy was that they hadn't even realised it.

Ashok was determined that this was not going to be him, even as he could feel the inexorable draw of the lull into withdrawal and entropy. "Not for Ashok," he resolved, "My parents did not make the Great Journey by steamer, leaving the huts of Gujarat as they set out for the English promised land, only for me to fall at the first hurdle and slip into comfortable oblivion." No, Ashok was a proud man and still had so much more to offer and to give to the world, in that he firmly believed.

* * * *

In Ashok we can see so many reflections of our own lives or the lives of people we know. Redundancy is a challenge that many of us may face at some point in our working lives; it can be a challenge that hits us hard. Equally, there is the hopeful if sometimes smug cliché of 'Losing my job was the best thing that ever happened to me.' Not specifically, you understand, but because of what it allowed the person then to go on and do. And it is this that gives the silver lining to the cloud of redundancy, when people are able to identify, realise and re-align their strengths in ways that they were not doing before — just as Ashok went on to do.

When Ashok digested his Realise2 report following his outplacement course, it had the same impact on him that Edison's discovery of the electric light bulb has had on the rest of us — where once there was darkness, now there was light: suddenly everything became clear and illuminated.

Ashok's strengths, it transpired, were in no way entirely out of keeping with his role at the bank, including Pride, Adherence, Work Ethic, Persistence, and Enabler. Yet his unrealised strengths told their own story of unfulfilled potential, and a life opportunity that without redundancy might otherwise have been missed. They were Mission, Legacy and Moral Compass. He had made his children his life's mission, but they had now grown up and so he was left wondering, and wandering. He had tried to convince himself that his legacy was served through helping the wealthy clients at the bank to increase their wealth even more. Now looking back, he could see what a lame excuse that had become. He had bought into the bank's mission, but had lost sight of his own.

Ashok thought back to a neighbourhood barbecue he had been at a couple of years before, where he had spoken to Harry, who, like him, had switched careers in his early fifties. In Harry's case, he moved from being a plumber (his knees eventually gave out) to becoming a church organ cleaner.

"A church organ cleaner?!" Ashok remembered thinking at the time, "You couldn't make it up!" But the life lessons imparted by Harry had stayed with him ever since: "If I had discovered this in my twenties, my life could have been so different!" had been the refrain with which Harry ended almost every sentence of their conversation.

As Harry had spoken, in between mouthfuls of slightly-charcoaled barbecue sausage, Ashok remembered that he felt something reverberate deep inside of him, not unlike the notes of a church organ. The sensation had stayed with him ever since, until now, grappling with redundancy and its aftermath, he finally felt as if he had been given the gift to do something about it.

Recognising this, on the "postcard to self" that Ashok completed as part of the outplacement course, he wrote: "I will have discovered who I am and what I want, and I will be doing (or well on the way to doing) what it is that I really want to do" had been Ashok's message to himself. He post-dated it for three months hence, allowing himself up to his leaving date to answer the questions he had set himself, find his direction, and make progress.

* * * *

It is almost three months later when we meet for the final time before Ashok leaves the bank. He has been asking himself the questions of who he wants to be and what he wants to do. In his quiet moments of reflection, he sits in his armchair overlooking the well-tended lawn of his back garden, etched out by a neat border with evenly spaced dahlias, primroses and pansies. A voice of ancient Indian wisdom floats through the air to him: "How do you want to be remembered?" it asks.

"To be remembered at all is enough" is his first reply, but then the spark of drive and ambition, implanted in him by his parents as they set out on the Great Journey, burns through his comfortable acquiescence and challenges him that he can — and should — do better: "I want to make a difference — and be remembered for doing so" is the answer that reverberates from deep within him.

"Now is the time to right some wrongs and do things differently," Ashok declares to me. "Yes, I can" he says, as if to himself, and in that moment, resolves that his second career is going to make more of a difference than his first ever did. Joining the ranks of many other financial services casualties of the Great Recession, Ashok opts for a career change that he believes will allow him to make more of a lasting and positive difference.

"I am going to join a financial literacy charity that educates people on how to deal with money more effectively, as well as lending them money at affordable rates so they can avoid the clutches of the loan-sharks and back-street lenders. At last I will be able to do the right thing, to give something back, and to do something that will make a real and lasting difference to people," Ashok grins, "The poacher has turned gamekeeper. It's time to put some justice back in the world."

"I really feel as if I have been given another chance," Ashok confesses to me, "as if I have woken up from a waking dream and I can do what I should be doing with my life — making a difference to people." The transformation is remarkable. "I just wish I had discovered this in my twenties," Ashok proclaims, "And my life could have been so different!"

"Indeed," I reply, "But the chances are that you were not ready for this in your twenties, Ashok. What you are now is the product of everything that you have become. Through your journey, you have been able to identify and realise the best of who you are. You likely weren't ready before, but now it is your time."

Whoever we are, when we find our strengths and realise the best of ourselves, it is our time.

* * * *

Ashok Shah found that he was able to reconnect with himself and be more effective in realising the best of himself through using his strengths. You can assess your own strengths use by completing the Strengths Use Scale which we have included for you below. There is also a downloadable version available at **www.strengths2020.com**.

THE STRENGTHS USE SCALE

The following questions ask you about your strengths, that is, the things that you are able to do well or do best. Please respond to each statement using the scale below:

1 Strongly disagree	2 Disagree	3 Slightly disagree	4 Neither agree or disagree	5 Slightly agree	6 Agree	7 Strongly agree

1. I am regularly able to do what I do best   _____

2. I always play to my strengths   _____

3. I always try to use my strengths   _____

4. I achieve what I want by using my strengths   _____

5. I use my strengths everyday   _____

6. I am able to use my strengths in lots of different situations   _____

7. I use my strengths to get what I want out of life   _____

8. My work gives me lots of opportunities to use my strengths   _____

9. My life presents me with lots of different ways to use my strengths _____

10. Using my strengths comes naturally to me   _____

11. I find it easy to use my strengths in the things I do   _____

12. Most of my time is spent doing things that I am
     good at doing   ____

13. Using my strengths is something I am familiar with ____

14. I am able to use my strengths in lots of different ways ____

How to score: Add up your responses to the 14 items. Higher scores indicate higher levels of strengths use. Strengths use is associated with better goal attainment, higher levels of happiness and well-being, and lower stress.

Source: Govindji, R., & Linley, P. A. (2007). Strengths use, self-concordance and well-being: Implications for strengths coaching and coaching psychologists. *International Coaching Psychology Review, 2* (2), 143–153. Reprinted with permission.

Strengths: The Evidence

Many of us will be familiar with the old adage "play to your strengths". In recent years, new research from the field of positive psychology and beyond has been providing the scientific underpinnings for why this matters and the benefits that using your strengths bring. Here is a summary of those benefits.

People who use their strengths more:

1. Are happier

2. Are more confident

3. Have higher levels of self-esteem

4. Have higher levels of energy and vitality

5. Experience less stress

6. Are more resilient

7. Are more likely to achieve their goals

8. Perform better at work

9. Are more engaged at work

10. Are more effective at developing themselves and growing as individuals.

But don't just take our word for it. If you want to read up on the evidence for this yourself, we've included all the sources for the original scientific research that led to these conclusions in Appendix 1. Check them out for yourself if you want to know more and see what the evidence shows about people who would regularly describe themselves as members of the list above.

For a downloadable version of *Strengths: The Evidence* visit **www.strengths2020.com**

Alex Linley's Top Ten Strengthspotting Tips

So you've read about Simon Lester, Jane Turner, Matt Johnson, Sara Stewart, and Ashok Shah. You know that using your strengths is a good thing to do, for at least ten reasons. But how do you know the strengths you have, and how can you identify them in other people? Well, you can take the online Realise2 strengths assessment (see **www.realise.com**), and you can also learn how to watch out for the telltale signs of a strength through Strengthspotting — do you remember the Strengthspotting Scale that you completed after reading about Simon Lester? Were you a natural strengthspotter or someone who needs some more practice?

In November 2008, I (Alex Linley) appeared on BBC One's The One Show. I was working with Tony Smith, a self-confessed pessimist, to see if I could help Tony to become more positive. One of the ways that I did this was through strengthspotting — helping Tony to identify the things he did well and loved to do. If you want to be a better strengthspotter, identifying strengths in yourself and in other people, these are our top ten things to watch out for. How many can you spot in yourself, or in the people around you?

1. **Childhood memories**: What do you remember doing as a child that you still do now — but most likely much better? Strengths often have deep roots from our early lives.

2. **Energy**: What activities give you an energetic buzz when you are doing them? These activities are very likely calling on your strengths.

3. **Authenticity**: When do you feel most like the "real you"? The chances are that you'll be using your strengths in some way.

4. **Ease**: See what activities come naturally to you, and at which you excel — sometimes, it seems, without even trying. These will likely be your strengths.

5. **Attention**: See where you naturally pay attention. You're more likely to focus on things that are playing to your strengths.

6. **Rapid learning:** What are the things that you have picked up quickly, learning them almost effortlessly? Rapid learning often indicates an underlying strength.

7. **Motivation:** What motivates you? When you find activities that you do simply for the love of doing them, they are likely to be working from your strengths.

8. **Voice:** Monitor your tone of voice. When you notice a shift in passion, energy and engagement, you're probably talking about a strength.

9. **Words and phrases:** Listen to the words you use. When you're saying "I love to..." or "It's just great when....," the chances are that it's a strength to which you're referring.

10. **"To do" lists:** Notice the things that never make it on to your "to do" list. These things that always seem to get done often reveal an underlying strength that means we never need to be asked twice.

For more information on strengthspotting, get the free download from **www.strengths2020.com**:

"Chapter 4: Strengthspotting"
An excerpt from
Average to A+: Realising Strengths in Yourself and Others,
by Alex Linley, published by CAPP Press, 2008.

Part Two
Realise2: Realising the Best of You

Realise2: Realising the Best of You

So far, you've met Simon Lester grappling with his people management challenges. You've resonated with Jane Turner as she strives to become who she is capable of becoming. You have felt the pain of Matt Johnson as he navigates the insecurities of parenthood. You've been tickled by Sara Stewart and her efforts to become a little bit more of an extrovert. And, depending on your age, you've either nervously looked ahead, or simultaneously shared the experiences of Ashok Shah as he finds a more rewarding career post-redundancy. You have seen how each of these people used their strengths to help them achieve what they wanted, to become who they wanted to become. In doing so, you've been introduced to some of the sixty strengths included in Realise2 (and which are explored further in Part 3).

Now it's time to turn our attention to the Realise2 model, and to understand exactly what we mean by strengths (whether realised or unrealised), learned behaviours and weaknesses. And — probably most important of all — it's time to get the "So what?" What should you do with all of this knowledge to make the difference you seek? This is where we are headed next.

What We *Actually* Mean by Strengths

When people talk about strengths, most people think about "the things that I'm good at". But actually, that's only half the answer — and it's the single biggest reason why so many people misunderstand strengths. As a result, they don't get the traction and performance that working from our strengths offers.

Think about this: Research has shown that only one in three people can say what their strengths are. Of these one in three people, the vast majority think their strengths are "the things that I'm good at." They miss what strengths are really about — and so they miss what strengths can do for them. And that's the people in the 33% of the population who have something of an idea to start with. The other 67% don't even get that far. But still, if you asked any of them, they would say that "My strengths are the things that I am good at." Half a point for that answer.

Okay, you've got the point (well, actually, half a point so far). So what's the other half of what a strength is that almost everyone is missing? Actually, it's simple. It's *energy*, the thing that makes the world go round (unlike love or money, despite the claims).

When you are using a strength, you feel energised. You get a buzz. You feel like it's the "real me" coming through. You feel like you could use the strength constantly and not need a pit-stop (but because of our physiological constraints, we do). It's the activity that has you leaping out of bed in the morning. It's the work assignment that has you screeching to a halt, leaving tyre marks in the office car park, because you can't get to your desk fast enough. It's that sense of "This is what I was born to do." Strengths are deeply fulfilling to us — and they should be. They are about our unique selves, who we are at our best.

In our academic research and our applied practice over the last ten years, we've spent thousands and thousands of person-hours interviewing people for strengths, reading about strengths, applying strengths practices in organisations, in schools, with individual people, in our own lives. We have been strengthspotting wherever we go and whatever we are doing — looking for the telltale signs of strengths in people and seeing the results that they achieve through using them.

As you've seen above in the section *Strengths: The Evidence*, these results are really worth taking note of. People perform better at work when they're using their strengths — and they're a lot more engaged with what they are doing. People are happier when they are using their strengths — and they feel more capable and more confident in what they can achieve. People grow, learn and develop best in the areas of their strengths — it's a fact, despite the apparently received "wisdom" that we should consider weaknesses to be synonymous with "areas for development".

Taking all of this work, and having read hundreds of research reports, books, conference abstracts and opinion pieces, we pulled all of our thinking together in the strengths book that precedes this one, *Average to A+: Realising Strengths in Yourself and Others*. If you haven't read it, do so. If we say it ourselves, it's worth it.

Based on all of these efforts, we've now established that strengths are defined by the presence of performance *and* energy. But there's also a critical third element — *use* — as we go on to explore below. First, though, let's debunk the myth that strengths are simply "the things that you are good at".

What We Don't Actually Mean by Strengths — Introducing Learned Behaviours

So, then, we've established that the two key elements of a strength are delivering a high level of *performance* and experiencing a sense of *energy* when you are doing it. If one of these is missing, it's not a strength. So what is it then? The answer is what we call a *learned behaviour*.

When you have performance *without* energy, over time, you will burn out. The satisfaction of a job well done, the positive reinforcement of pats-on-the-back, the little voice that continues in telling you that you have to keep on doing it. Even worse, the voice that says these are your (misidentified) strengths, so just stick with them. Over time, the impact of all of this runs out. They're simply not sustainable — they're learned behaviours.

> **Learned behaviours are the things at which you perform well, but which you find de-energising or draining. Over time, they will lead to burn-out if not used in moderation.**

These learned behaviours come about through precisely this combination of being good at something, and having the positive reinforcement that comes from being good at it. Unfortunately, they're missing the energy component that makes them sustainable.

When we're being asked to do it by a superior, and being rewarded for our good performance through using the learned behaviour, we fall into the trap of thinking, "Well, I should do this, because it is playing to my [misidentified] strengths."

We then become totally confused when we feel burned out and exhausted, thinking that we have been playing to our strengths, like all the best advice argues: "There must be something wrong with me, I must have got it wrong."

The good news is that, yes, you got it wrong. But no, there's nothing wrong with you — you're just like the other 99.999% of the population who think that a strength is "something I'm good at" without recognising that it is also "something that energises me." And that's easily fixed — we wrote this book and developed Realise2 to help people just like you.

When you understand strengths as being about the combination of performance *and* energy, you can differentiate them from learned behaviours — performance *without* energy. Making this critical distinction, you're well on the way to *really* understanding yourself and what it takes for you to be at your best — sustainably, over the long term.

Why It's Not *Just* All About Strengths — Introducing Weaknesses

We've seen that the big differentiator between strengths and learned behaviours is *energy*. But there's also another part to this — what happens when we introduce poor performance into the equation? This is where weaknesses come into play. Weaknesses are the things where you perform poorly at the same time as you are drained or de-energised by them — a pretty debilitating combination, which makes you wonder why we would ever use them in the first place.

> Weaknesses are the things at which you both perform poorly and find de-energising or draining. When weaknesses are used, they lead to feelings of negativity, disengagement, and lack of motivation.

If a weakness is de-energising and something you're no good at doing, why on earth would you be doing it in the first place? The usual reasons are the result of some combination of our negativity bias (through evolution, we naturally attend to what's wrong), faulty assumptions about human nature (we wrongly assume that everyone will develop best through practicing their weaknesses), poor job design (the job spec was written based on the last person who did it, rather than what needs to be done), and bad management (all of the above coming together in an unfortunate individual who has management responsibilities).

Fortunately, most of us manage to avoid this quite naturally for a lot of the time — and the best performers manage to do it even better than the rest of us. Sometimes, though, we get sucked into doing things that we don't enjoy, feel drained by, and at which we perform badly. We look below at what you need to do about this.

Adding the Third Lens — Strengths Use — To Distinguish Between Realised and Unrealised Strengths

Energy helps us to distinguish between strengths, and learned behaviours and weaknesses: strengths are energising, learned behaviours and weaknesses are not. *Performance* helps to distinguish between weaknesses, and strengths and learned behaviours: we perform well using strengths and learned behaviours, we perform poorly using our weaknesses.

There is also a third lens we can apply to understand things even further: *use*. If a weakness isn't being used, it's not a problem. If a learned behaviour isn't being used, it's not a problem. But what about if a strength isn't being used — what does that mean?

Adding the lens of *strengths use*, we distinguish between realised strengths and unrealised strengths. Realised strengths are the strengths we are most likely to recognise, because we will be using them more frequently.

> Realised strengths are the things which you perform well at, find energising, and do frequently.

In contrast, unrealised strengths may be new to us, because we don't have the situation or opportunity to use them as much. This distinction between realised strengths and unrealised strengths is a powerful one. Quite simply, *our areas of greatest potential for development exist in our unrealised strengths*. Realised strengths, by definition, are already being used to good effect in achieving good performance results — and we may overstep the mark and go too far by focusing on them even more (see below on overplayed strengths).

In contrast, unrealised strengths are, by definition, not being used so much — and yet they are the things that energise us and at which we could excel. As a result, there is far more room for growth and development in our areas of unrealised strengths — but until now, this distinction has not been made. See Appendix 2 at the end of the book for a sample personal development plan, which you could use to help you in developing your own strengths, whether realised or unrealised.

> Unrealised strengths are the things at which you perform well, find energising, but don't do very much.

The Realise2 Model

From this distinction, Realise2 was born. *Realise* means, first, to see, to identify, to recognise and to understand. Realise also means, second, to bring into being, to make manifest, to make real, or to bring to fruition. *Realise2* is about both these two meanings of realise: to know what our strengths are and to realise the potential inherent within them. It's why we gave *Average to A+* the subtitle of *Realising Strengths in Yourself and Others*.

We use the term Realise2 to refer to both a model of effective individual and organisational development, and also our online assessment and development tool (visit **www.strengths2020.com** if you haven't yet taken it), based on the three dimensions of energy, performance and use:

> **Energy** — how energising you find an activity;
> **Performance** — how good you are at doing an activity;
> **Use** — how often you actually do the activity.

These three dimensions of energy, performance and use combine in different ways to produce realised and unrealised strengths, learned behaviours and weaknesses. This holistic model gives a much more comprehensive and integrated way of understanding who we are as individual human beings, of understanding why we do what we do, and of understanding the areas where we will shine and where we will struggle. You can see how the model fits together in Figure 1, the Realise2 Quadrant Model. Next, we go on to look at how you can achieve optimal performance, through making the most of your strengths, moderating your learned behaviours, and minimising your weaknesses.

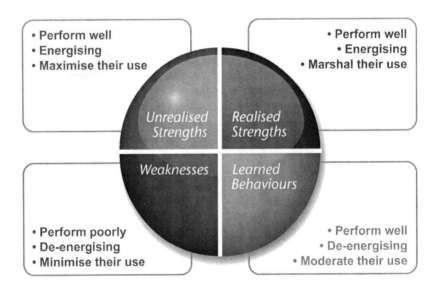

Figure 1. The Realise2 Quadrant Model

Minimise Weaknesses to Make them Irrelevant

As we established above, weaknesses are de-energising and we're poor at delivering performance when using them. So why do we? The reasons are typically as we discussed: the mis-organisation of organisations that are still failing to follow Peter Drucker's prescient advice that "...the unique purpose of organization is to make strength productive...and make weaknesses irrelevant." Think about it — we don't ever tend to use our weaknesses too much at home — it always seems to be at work, following patterns that have unfortunately been laid down too often while we were at school.

This is because instead of following Drucker's advice, most places are still fixated on "developing weaknesses" — with the collusion of the misguided intention of performance reviews and school reports that dress up weaknesses by mislabelling them as "areas for development".

Let's be clear on two things. First, a weakness is a weakness — so let's call it that and accept it as such. This isn't necessarily an easy thing to do, but it can make a big difference. Accepting a weakness as such means that we can get on with dealing with it and focusing our development attention elsewhere. It also means that we can ask for help where we need it, and be more honest about the work and roles that we are suited for and those we are not — avoiding a lot of stress in the process.

Second, an "area for development" should be something where you can develop to become really good, if not fantastic — and that's not ever going to be in an area of weakness. For sure, the negative impact of weaknesses needs to be minimised and the weaknesses themselves need to be made irrelevant so that they're not undermining performance — *but that's all*. We shouldn't be wasting people's time on trying to make people excel in things at which they are inherently poor.

The only people who benefit from weakness development programmes are consultants, because they keep being asked back time and again to try and fix their interventions that haven't worked. It's certainly not the people being developed who benefit, who are not only wasting their time, but being made to feel like failures in the process. Nor, paradoxically, is it the purchasers of this development — typically organisations or schools, but sometimes the individuals themselves. This is the myth of weakness development, and it's been around for too long.

Any development focused exclusively on weaknesses is, quite

simply, wrong. We shouldn't be focused on developing weaknesses, we should be focused on minimising them. Instead of this perennial sadly-go-round of weakness development, we need to know what our weaknesses are, and then to manage them in a way that makes them minimised and their impact irrelevant. The belief that developing our weaknesses will make us star performers is one of the great myths of the modern age, and it's time it was debunked.

This is how to minimise your weaknesses and their impact:

- *Reshape the role*: Can you re-shape what you do? Try to reorganise what you do in a way that reduces the extent to which you have to use the weakness, ideally to the extent that you don't have to do it at all. Do this by delegating to others — if you can — or by re-arranging the way that work gets done.
- *Use strengths to compensate*: Can you use or apply one or more of your strengths in such a way that your weakness is compensated for? For example, a strength in Personal Responsibility might enable a weakness in Planful to be overcome.
- *Find a complementary partner:* Can you work with someone else who has a strength, and performs strongly, where you have a weakness? Try to find someone who can compensate for you, someone who has strength where you have weakness. In return, do something for them that they struggle with and that you do well.
- *Adopt strengths-based team working*: Can you re-organise how things are done using a "team strengths" rather than "task-led" approach? Try to re-allocate tasks, objectives or responsibilities according to the strengths of individuals. When an approach like this is working at its best, every member of the team, in effect, works as a complementary partner to other team members.
- *Undertake training/development to mitigate the weakness*: If none of the above are possible, can you learn to practice this weakness to a level of competence? Recognise and learn to accept that the weakness is not something you're ever likely to do well or be energised by. Instead, aim to be as good as you need to be — in other words *good enough*, so that the weakness is minimised and no longer undermines your overall performance.

Figure 2. Minimise Weaknesses to Make Them Irrelevant

Moderating Learned Behaviours for Sustainable Performance

We've seen how to deal with weaknesses in order to make them irrelevant. But what about learned behaviours? After all, they are things that we actually do well, it's just that they are de-energising over time. As such, the best advice is about using learned behaviours as appropriate and as needed, while recognising that they won't ever be the royal road to sustainable high performance. By doing this, we can ensure that our lives don't become dominated by learned behaviours, thereby robbing us of the chance to flourish through using our strengths.

Here's how you can moderate your learned behaviours for sustainable performance:

- *Stop doing it*: Can you just stop using the learned behaviour? If your learned behaviour use has simply become ingrained and automatic, you may be able to stop without any detrimental impact on your role or wider responsibilities. If so, you'll make space to use your strengths more, with all the benefits that brings.

- *Refocus the role*: Can you re-focus what you do? Try to re-organise what you do in a way that reduces the extent to which you have to use the learned behaviour, ideally so that you can play more to your real strengths.
- *Organise tasks and activities into "strengths sandwiches"*: Can you be more mindful of how and when you complete less energising activities? Try to create a better balance by sandwiching activities that drain you by using your learned behaviours between more energising activities that play to your strengths.
- *Find a complementary partner*: Can you work with someone who has strengths in areas such that they get energised where you get de-energised — even if you both performed the same? Find someone who would be energised by taking on the things that you get drained by. In return, do something for them that they struggle with, which will help performance for both of you to be sustainable over time.

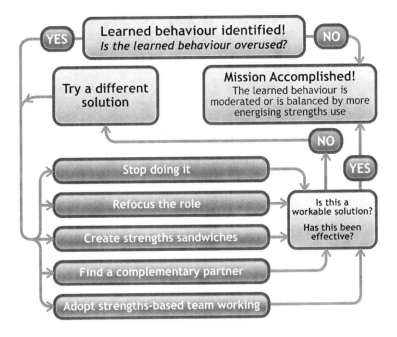

Figure 3. Moderate Learned Behaviours for Sustainable Performance

- *Adopt strengths-based team working*: Can you re organise how things are done using a "team strengths" rather than "task-led" approach? Try to reallocate tasks, objectives or responsibilities according to what people are energised by, rather than only what they do well. This will require an honest dialogue from everyone about whether they truly enjoy the things they may, in the past, have been recognised for, yet weren't energised by.

Marshal Realised Strengths for Optimal Performance

Having managed our weaknesses and moderated our learned behaviours, we should also be ensuring that we get the best from our strengths through making them productive. Here's how to achieve optimal performance through marshalling your realised strengths:

- *Understand your strengths*: First and foremost, we need to know and understand what our strengths are — really understand them. That means not confusing them with learned behaviours, or things that we enjoy but never have a chance of being really good at. To really understand our strengths means identifying those activities at which we excel and which make us feel energised. Only then will we really be prepared to put in the long hours and heavy effort needed for making a strength truly great.
- *Harness strengths to goals*: Strengths are always strengths in context, never in isolation. There's no point having Personalisation if there are no people around, or Planful if there's nothing to plan. To harness your strengths to best effect, you need to be clear on what you are harnessing them to. What are your goals? What are your objectives? What do you want to achieve? Having answered these questions, you can then start to look at how your strengths will be able to help you make progress and achieve what you want.
- *Use your strengths to compensate*: We have already highlighted that one particularly valuable way in which strengths can be deployed is to use them to compensate for learned behaviours and weaknesses. Having a weakness in Detail can be overcome through harnessing a strength in Pride. Personal Responsibility can be used to compensate for Planful. Any number of compensating strengths combinations exist. Which ones are open to you with your unique pattern of strengths, weaknesses and learned behaviours?
- *Combine strengths for multiplier effect*: We don't just have one or two strengths, but rather a symphony of strengths on which we can call. What do your strengths look like in combination, and how

does this play out in the context of what you want to achieve? As one simple example, Competitive paired with Compassion looks very different to Competitive paired with Drive. Finding the right combinations of strengths can lead to multiplier effects, whereby you transform your capable to achieve through using two or more strengths together.

- *Calibrate*: *Don't overplay strengths*: Strengths overplayed can lead to catastrophic declines in performance, so we need to be careful to calibrate effectively. Pay attention to your situation and context, making sure to use the strength to the right amount. Strengths do not have an on/off switch, but rather a volume control: we can turn them up or turn them down as appropriate for the situation. If you're unsure yourself, collecting honest feedback from those around you is a reliable way to calibrate your strengths, keeping them appropriately used and optimally aligned to what you are striving to achieve.

- *Monitor and refine*: Having put together your strengths action plan, put it into practice and see how you get on. What is working? What isn't? Are you harnessing the most effective combinations of strengths to compensate for your weaknesses and learned behaviours? Strengths use is always a journey, never a destination.

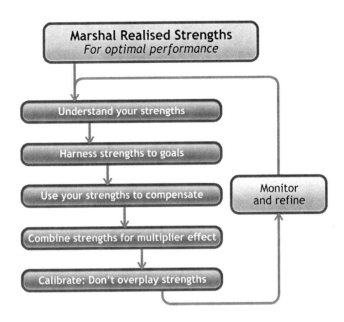

Figure 4. Marshal Realised Strengths for Optimal Performance

Evaluation and refinement are critical and should be constant companions as you work towards goal attainment through your strengths.

Maximise Unrealised Strengths for Growth and Development

If we are to make the most of our strengths, and particularly if we want to turbo-charge our growth and development, we need to pay attention to our unrealised strengths. These will be the strengths that, for whatever reason, we may not have been using so much. They represent deep wells of potential that rest within us, and from which we can draw as we seek to develop ourselves and our abilities.

- *Identify your unrealised strengths*: It may not be easy to identify your unrealised strengths, because sometimes you may not know that they are there. There are, however, a number of ways to do this. Most obviously, you can complete Realise2. You can also pay attention to things that you may have a yearning to do, or that you do in your leisure as hobbies or pastimes, since these are the things that you *choose* to do — and this can be an indicator of a nascent strength. Further, think about who you admire and why you admire them. Sometimes we look up to our heroes and heroines because they do things we cannot; other times, it's because they do something that resonates with us and that we think we might be able to improve in ourselves.
- *Find the need/opportunity*: By definition, an unrealised strength is not being used very much, and this may reflect the fact that you are lacking the need or the opportunity to use it. If so, what can you do to change this? Of course, just trying things out can be a motivation that creates the opportunity in itself, but you might also want to explore linking your unrealised strengths to tasks that need to be done, at home or at work, or to hobbies or pastimes that will provide you with a safe environment to experiment with your new behaviours.
- *Practise, practise, practise*: As we start using a new strength, we need to practise it. We are likely to experience rapid learning when we practise using a strength, and this can be a very good indicator that we have accurately identified an unrealised strength in ourselves. If so, the practice will never be onerous, but rather a pleasurable opportunity to master a new way of working that will serve us in many different ways.

- *Develop and hone*: Our practice, however, can only get us so far. To really develop an unrealised strength to the full, we might also need to bring in particular learning and development. This could take the shape of formal courses or programmes, or more on-the-job experience. We may pay close attention to people who already display the strength far better than we do, studying them to see what we can learn and emulate from their example. In doing so, we will never simply be making copycat reproductions of them, since we'll also be learning how the strength plays out uniquely for us, and what we can do to ensure that we get the best from it while being at our most authentic.
- *Expand and extend your reach*: Over time, with practice and development, the unrealised strength will become realised: we will be using it more, and becoming more successful in doing so. As this happens, we can then turn our attention to where we go and what we do with it next. Can we expand the repertoire of our strength, taking on bigger or more complex activities that require us to use it? Can we extend it into new situations and environments, trying out our new behaviours with a variety of

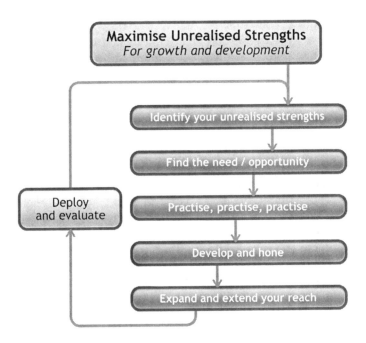

Figure 5. Maximise Unrealised Strengths for Growth and Development

opportunities that give us the opportunity to test, explore and develop. We will never know unless we try.

- **Deploy and evaluate**: Finally, as we work our way through all of these steps for developing our unrealised strengths, we should constantly be testing our ideas through the crucible of experience: deploying the strength in practice and evaluating how we get on. Did we get the results we expected? What have we learned along the way? What can we improve as we move forward with developing this strength? These are the questions to which we should periodically return, in order to truly optimise our growth and development through maximising our unrealised strengths.

Strengths Overplayed

Lots of the existing advice around strengths encourages people to "use your strengths more". But practical experience shows that that isn't always the solution — and in some cases, it can be quite the wrong advice — becoming a derailer, rather than an enabler.

Why? The thing that so many people have missed, or simply got wrong, is to think that because a strength is "something you are good at" then it makes sense to do it more. This "do it more" advice misses two big and important caveats.

First, we need to remember that strengths are about performance and energy. This can be a pretty lethal combination for strengths becoming overplayed. Given that strengths are energising and we're good at them, we can easily be tempted into taking them too far — and overplayed strengths can lead to our downfall with catastrophic declines in performance.

Second, it's important to know your context and need. What is it appropriate to do in the situation and context in which you find yourself? This is especially true when the context or need has changed. We have seen many people who are great in one situation, but not in another. And the challenge is that because it has worked once, people think that it will work again. And when it doesn't, they think they should just do it even more. Better situational judgement is essential, and people don't always have it. The key is to know how much of any given strength to use at any given time.

We call it the Golden Mean of Strengths Use. It's easy to say and easy to remember, but less easy to put into practice. In fact, Aristotle coined a word around this whole concept — *phronesis* — which can be loosely translated as "practical wisdom". It's about having the situational judgement to know what to do, when, and to what extent — and there's a whole other book to be written on this concept (but we'll leave that one for the future).

Now You Know: The Four Things You Need to Do

Now you know the crucial difference between a strength and a learned behaviour, and hopefully you can also spot a weakness a mile off and know what to do about it. What else is there that you might need to know?

First, you need to know your strengths and understand how they can best work in combination with each other to help you to achieve your goals and objectives. Importantly, you also need to understand your situation and context, which you will do by deploying your strengths and evaluating how you get on. Marshal your realised strengths, being careful not to take them too far, which we think of as the Golden Mean of Strengths Use: Use the right strength, to the right amount, in the right way and at the right time.

Second, start focusing your growth and development in a direction that will make a difference. Pay attention to unrealised strengths that could provide you with an opportunity to try out new strengths combinations, or develop abilities you never knew you had. Maximising your unrealised strengths will help you to unlock a higher level of performance by tapping your unrealised potential.

Third, hopefully by now we've said enough to raise the red warning flag of over-used learned behaviours to you. These can be deceptively deceiving — we're good at doing them, rewarded for doing them, and even internalise them as our (misidentified) strengths — and then we become exhausted and burned out through doing them too much and wonder why. Follow the advice above and moderate learned behaviours for maximum performance and sustainability.

Fourth, we've hopefully done enough to convince you to stop and think again before you start calling weaknesses "areas for development," and to stop assuming that that's where all the learning and development budget should be spent. And if we haven't, put the book down now, go and take a very cold shower, and come back and start reading again from page 1.

Yes, weaknesses should very legitimately be minimised and made irrelevant so that they are not undermining performance. No, they should not become our exclusive development focus, because (a) we'll never be that good at them, (b) excessive weakness development is a waste of money, and (c) focusing excessively on weaknesses leaves people feeling really bad about themselves — and that's not good for them, for their performance, or for your business.

Together, these give you the four things you need to do:

> **The Four Things You Need to Do:**
>
> 1. Marshal realised strengths for optimal performance
> 2. Maximise unrealised strengths for growth and development
> 3. Moderate learned behaviours for sustainable performance
> 4. Minimise weaknesses to make them irrelevant

If you do each of these four things, you will be well on the road to lasting high performance. And if you're a manager or a leader practising them in your organisation, you'll be well on the way to enabling your people to give you the levels of engagement, energy and performance that you always suspected were there, but never quite managed to tap into. Congratulations.

What This Means for You — As an Individual, As a Manager, As a Parent

You've read this far, and we've given you the crux of what we wanted you to know. To make it even easier — and as a quick reference guide for when you're on the go, or, if you're only scanning through the book, because we know that you'll like bullet points better — here's the headline summary of what this means for you as an individual, as a manager, and as a parent.

Realising the Best of You as an Individual:

- Don't confuse strengths with learned behaviours. Strengths are about what we're good at (performance) AND what we find energising (energy) — performance without energy is a learned behaviour.
- Don't overplay strengths by taking them too far. Equally, be sure to moderate your learned behaviours and to manage your weaknesses — Figures 2 and 3 above will help you do this.
- Remember that your greatest well-being, your greatest development, and your greatest performance come from using your strengths — not from relying on your learned behaviours or struggling along trying to make your weaknesses great.

- Your strengths can be realised strengths (that you use frequently) or unrealised strengths (that you don't use much). Your truly greatest areas for development are in the area of your unrealised strengths, as Figure 5 shows.
- Realise2 helps you to identify your realised strengths, unrealised strengths, learned behaviours and weaknesses. Having done so, you can use the development suggestions provided as well as creating your own development plan – all online. Visit **www.realise2.com** You can also find a sample personal development plan in Appendix 2 at the end of the book.

Realising the Best of You as a *Manager*:

- Don't confuse your employees' learned behaviours with their strengths. You'll be used to looking for good performance, but we're telling you that performance is not enough. If you want performance to be sustainable, and you want to create an engaged and happy workforce that is the envy of your peers and the pride of your bosses, identify your employees' strengths. Then help them to harness them to the full in delivering your team objectives and corporate strategy.
- Stop wasting your organisation's money, your employees' engagement, and your own valuable time on trying to make people great in their areas of weakness. Minimise weaknesses to make them irrelevant, by all means, but *please* stop trying to make people great at their weaknesses. It just won't happen and you risk doing a lot of damage along the way.
- Recognise that the well-rounded individual of competency frameworks is an absolute myth. All that we have created in trying to find them is an organisational sea of mediocrity where everyone sinks to the lowest common competency denominator, rather than being allowed to shine to their highest potential.
- Understand and leverage your role as a climate engineer for your team. As the manager, what you do has impact – whether you recognise it or not. As the saying goes, "When the leader sneezes, the organisation catches a cold." It's the same for you as a manager. If you sneeze your team catches a cold. Use your climate control to create the team environment of which you can be proud. Identify people's strengths as enablers of performance, and reward them for that performance (*not* for just using their strengths).

- Become the Super Strengthspotter of your team and catch people doing things well. Teach yourself the Top Ten Strengthspotting Tips and see what strengths you can spot in your team on an ongoing basis. Not only will you create a powerfully positive climate through that individual recognition, you'll also be much better equipped in knowing who should do what when it comes to task allocation and team working.

Realising the Best of You as a *Parent*:

- When you see your child doing something well, stop and ask yourself if you also see the energy that would suggest it's a strength. Or are you at risk of ingraining a learned behaviour because you are rewarding them (praise, a pat on the back, a chocolate bar, or a trip to the zoo) for something that they do well, but that isn't a strength?.
- Don't panic! We don't want you now to become paranoid about what you reward. Remember, our brain wiring is laid down over many years throughout childhood and adolescence, so the praise and reward that you gave for learned behaviours before you read this book can be undone. And don't worry, your children will have their own sense of what is right for them and what isn't, where their strengths lie and where they don't. Things only get distorted when learned behaviours are ingrained, or weaknesses are the predominant focus, over a period of years.
- When you do see that spark of greatness in your child, try planting a "golden seed". A kind word here, a pat on the back there, a hug of encouragement somewhere else…if these golden seeds are sown in the fertile ground of a nascent strength, they could sustain your child for a lifetime.
- Remember that academic success is not everything, that there are many ways to be successful in life. If your child doesn't succeed in one area, they'll likely be able to shine somewhere else. Your job as a parent is to help them explore those options and find what's right for them. Praise effort rather than attainment to help them develop a growth mindset.
- Above all else, love your children for who and what they are. You created them and they will hopefully carry your genes and your legacy into the future. Act so that you can be proud of who you are as a parent, and proud of who they are as the children you have raised.

Part Three
The Realise2 Strengths

How to Use this Strengths Library

Over the pages that follow we will introduce you to each of the sixty Realise2 strengths in more detail, with each one illustrated with examples and suggestions for use. We use a number of standard conventions — everything from symbols representing the strengths to descriptions of real life people who demonstrate the strengths. In every case, these conventions are designed to provide a deeper understanding of the strengths and to act as a guide for you to recognise and use the strengths even better yourself.

Each of the entries in the strengths library is made up of eleven elements. The section below explains what these elements are, and how to get the best from them.

Strengths Symbol — This is the symbol that represents the strength — see the "Strengths Symbology" chapter for a fuller description of strengths symbology in general, and each symbol in particular.

Strength Name — This is the name of the strength. For example, it might read "Action" or "Moral Compass" or any of the 58 other entries. Below we use "Action" as the example.

Brief Strength Definition — This provides a quick, easy reference overview of what the strength is.

If You Have a Strength in Action — A fuller description of how the strength will play out for people who have it.

The Action Catchphrase — The catchphrase you might expect to hear from people with this strength. Listen out for it and see what other catchphrases you notice.

Meet Jane, Strong in Action — A story about the strength that is taken from one of our thousands of strengths interviews with people.

Action Hall of Fame — Public figures who we believe demonstrate this strength. These figures are men and women, from the past to the present day, across a wide variety of walks of life, whose achievements evidence the strength in question.

Action in Relationships — Headline advice on how this strength plays out in relationships, including what works well and what to watch out for if you have this strength.

Action at Work — Here we make suggestions for occupations where your strength could find a good fit at work. This is, however, a broad-brush approach. Successful careers depend on more than one strength being a match for the role, as our work in strengths-based recruitment shows.

Action at Play — Here we suggest leisure activities that you might enjoy if you have this strength. Give them a go and see how you get on!

But Don't Take it Too Far — Finally, we sound the note of caution for each strength. The golden mean of strengths use is critical — "the right strength, to the right amount, in the right way, and at the right time". So, here we provide some cautionary guidance about ensuring you don't take your strengths too far, but instead use them for optimal sustainable performance.

The Realise2 Strengths

Action

People strong in Action feel compelled to act immediately and decisively.

If You Have a Strength in Action...

You feel an overriding compulsion to act immediately and decisively. You are much more comfortable with forward momentum than you are with careful strategy and reflection. As soon as you get an idea you don't want to wait. Getting started is the only way for you. You take the attitude that if it works then fantastic, but if it doesn't then at least you had a try.

The Action Catchphrase...

"Let's get going!"

Meet Jane, strong in Action...

"Why wait? If I get a great idea or someone else comes to me with an idea, I want to act on it straight away. I seem to have a surplus of energy and often feel as if I am compelled to act. It happened earlier on today, my digital artist rang, he had some great ideas on how to improve the pictures that he was working on. But he needed input from both me and other people. I got the call from him at 10.00 and as soon as I put the phone down I was on the case. In the following 10 minutes I had enlisted the help of two other people so that his idea could be implemented. Getting started is the only way, I don't want to sit on it, take things slowly and think about it. I have made some mistakes jumping in this way I suppose, but at least we have known quickly about them and we put them right quickly. I find it aggravating if the planning stage takes too long or if the people I work with work slowly."

Action Hall of Fame...

- **Bob Geldof** — Irish singer who rose to fame with the Boomtown Rats; later known for his political activism, which started when he formed Band Aid to raise money to provide famine relief for Ethiopia.

- **Angelina Jolie** — Oscar-winning Hollywood actress, perhaps best known for starring as Lara Croft in the action-packed *Tomb Raider* films.
- **Freya Stark** — One of the first Western women to travel through the Arabian deserts; famous for her experiences in the Middle East, her travel writing, and her map making.

Action in Relationships — What Works and What to Watch Out For...

You are likely to want to engage heavily in your relationships. This may mean you have a higher expectation of physical affection, the desire to confront conflict, or the need to feel like you are sharing your experiences with those around you. Allow other people their space, since not everyone will be as oriented to action as you are.

Action at Work — Occupations Where You Could Find a Fit...

- Accident and Emergency worker;
- Bar/restaurant manager;
- Construction worker;
- Military personnel;
- Political organiser.

Action at Play — Leisure Suggestions You Might Enjoy...

- Go-kart racing;
- Martial arts;
- Role playing;
- Theatre;
- Video games.

But Don't Take It Too Far...Action Overplayed...

Don't let your forward momentum cause you to crash! Your strength in acting quickly, decisively, and without hesitation can, if overplayed, result in you leading others down the wrong path. Leave sufficient space to pause, reflect, and take stock.

Adherence

People strong in Adherence like to follow processes, operating firmly within rules and guidelines.

If You Have a Strength in Adherence...

You have a natural focus on taking the right approach. You love following guidelines, rules, instructions and procedures. You feel most comfortable completing tasks that have clear steps and stages, where you are trusted — and expected — to follow these steps and stages to the letter.

The Adherence Catchphrase...

"Rules are there to be followed."

Meet Charles, strong in Adherence...

"There is no question about me deviating from the rules. If the rulebook says it has to be done in such a way, then it must say it for a reason. Rules are there to be followed to the letter and that is what I do — I follow them to the letter. Actually, I do tend to go for jobs where there is some strict structure in place. I work better that way — I know what I am supposed to do and people know what to expect from me."

Adherence Hall of Fame...

- **Warren Buffett** — American billionaire and philanthropist; Chairman of Berkshire Hathaway, recognised for having the same daily routine for decades.

- **Queen Elizabeth II** — British monarch since her coronation in 1953, recognised for her adherence to her coronation oath and the appropriate decorum of her public office.

- **Vanessa Mae** — British music star; classically trained musician who successfully fuses classical and modern forms of music.

Adherence in Relationships — What Works and What to Watch Out For...

You are likely to be influenced by traditional social roles and may be uncomfortable when these are threatened. You are more likely to create habits and patterns in the way you relate to others. This can help people to feel safe and secure in their dealings with you, but allow yourself time for spontaneity as well!

Adherence at Work — Occupations Where You Could Find a Fit...

- Air traffic controller;
- Legal secretary;
- Tax inspector;
- Traffic warden;
- Train driver.

Adherence at Play — Leisure Suggestions You Might Enjoy...

- Bonsai tree growing;
- Genealogy;
- Matchstick modelling;
- Sewing/knitting;
- Tea ceremony.

But Don't Take It Too Far...Adherence Overplayed...

Don't stifle progress! Your strength in following guidelines, rules, instructions, and procedures and following steps and stages to the letter can, if overplayed, hinder innovation. Allow space, when necessary, for the creative process to unfold — rules need sometimes to be tested and broken for new ones to emerge.

Adventure

People strong in Adventure like to take risks and stretch themselves outside their comfort zone.

If You Have a Strength in Adventure...

You relish the risk of the unusual or the untried. You look forward to experiences that are on the edge of, or outside, your comfort zone. You like to see how you would react to new and difficult situations. New and challenging scenarios provide ways for you to test yourself, to understand what you can and can't do, to gain personal insights, and to prove yourself. Above all, you love to push the boundaries and see what life will throw at you.

The Adventure Catchphrase...

"I'll try it..."

Meet Robert, strong in Adventure...

"I love to travel to different places, places that people wouldn't normally associate with going on holiday. I find that I am pretty comfortable with being uncomfortable. I find it exciting to do something that scares me and that carries a real risk. I don't mean real danger, like I would never deliberately go into a war zone or anything like that — but I mean something that takes me to the edge. I even find myself wondering what I would do if I was placed in certain scenarios, I might not like them but I want to see how I would react to them. They would be a test of what I can and can't do and give me a deeper knowledge and understanding of myself."

Adventure Hall of Fame...

- **Louise Arner Boyd** — American who inherited her family's wealth at age 13 and then travelled around Europe; Arctic explorer and the first woman to fly over the North Pole in 1955.

- **Christopher Columbus** — 15th Century Italian sea navigator and explorer; widely credited with the modern European discovery of the Americas.

* **Valentina Tereshkova** — Soviet cosmonaut and pilot of Vostok 6 in June 1963, in doing so becoming the first woman to go into space.

Adventure in Relationships — What Works and What to Watch Out For...

You are likely to want to actively experience the world with those around you. You seek out new and challenging experiences and may become bored easily in relationships. Be careful that your need for adventure doesn't alienate the people around you who might still want to invest in the relationship, but don't have the appetite for risk or adventure as much as you do.

Adventure at Work — Occupations Where You Could Find a Fit...

* Firefighter;
* Humanitarian aid worker;
* Outdoor pursuits instructor;
* Reporter;
* Tour operator.

Adventure at Play — Leisure Suggestions You Might Enjoy...

* Canoeing;
* Fantasy role play;
* Hang gliding;
* Jungle trekking;
* Travel.

But Don't Take It Too Far...Adventure Overplayed...

Don't become an adrenaline junkie! Your strength in stretching yourself outside your comfort zone and testing yourself in new and unfamiliar situations can, if overplayed, mean that you never settle to anything for any length of time. It will also impact negatively on your health, well-being, and relationships. Learn to balance your need for adventure with a capacity for more routine activity. Make sure you also balance your need to stretch yourself with your wider life needs and interests.

Authenticity

People strong in Authenticity are always true to themselves, even in the face of pressure from others.

If You Have a Strength in Authenticity...

Whatever you do, you do it with genuine feeling and without pretence. You always keep to your own values and beliefs, no matter what people want you to do. Indeed, regardless of pressure from others, you are proud to stand up for what you believe in, doing the things that are right for you, in the way that is right for you.

The Authenticity Catchphrase...

"I am who I am."

Meet Zach, strong in Authenticity...

"I am known for my integrity, people know that I will always follow the path that is right for me and aligned to my values. I just can't think about behaving in any other way. It doesn't always go down well with friends, though, like the other evening when I went to a quiz night with some people I know. I love quizzes and the competitive person in me wants to win. But not at any cost. I was appalled when the group I was with pulled out a mobile phone to help with the answers. It didn't matter what I said, though they didn't see anything wrong with what they were doing, and still referred to the phone. In the end, I didn't want anything to do with them or the situation. So I got up and quietly left, I just couldn't bear to be in a situation like this which went against the grain of who I am and what I believe in."

Authenticity Hall of Fame...

- **Cheryl Cole** — Girls Aloud singer and X Factor judge; grew up in a deprived inner city council estate in Newcastle-upon-Tyne, but rose to prominence through ITV talent show *Popstars: The Rivals*.

- **General Bernard Montgomery** — Second World War era British general; credited with major victories in North Africa and Italy; outspoken critic of practices with which he did not agree.

- **Michael Moore** — Documentary film maker and Academy Award winner; has a reputation for politically liberal views and the ability to confront public scrutiny.

Authenticity in Relationships — What Works and What to Watch Out For...

You are likely to place a high premium on honesty. This means that you have a tendency to demand that others accept you as you are and that you expect others to be forthright in being themselves in return. You are unlikely to tolerate people who you think are false or acting out a role.

Authenticity at Work — Occupations Where You Could Find a Fit...

- Artist;
- Entrepreneur;
- Journalist;
- Psychotherapist;
- Scholar.

Authenticity at Play — Leisure Suggestions You Might Enjoy...

- Astronomy;
- Mentoring young people;
- Reading;
- The arts;
- Volunteering.

But Don't Take It Too Far...Authenticity Overplayed...

Know when to insist on being yourself, as well as learning when it's okay to flex a little! Your strength in behaving in a way that is in keeping with what you believe in can, if overplayed, jar with the situation. Know when and in what context it is right to bring your Authenticity to the fore, and in what measure.

Bounceback

People strong in Bounceback use setbacks as springboards to go on and achieve even more.

If You Have a Strength in Bounceback...

Whatever the obstacle, setback, or disappointment you come up against, it just makes you more determined to succeed. Following disappointments, you love to pick yourself up very quickly and use setbacks as a springboard to spur you on, to prove yourself and to achieve more than you would have done otherwise.

The Bounceback Catchphrase...

"Knock me down and I'll come back stronger."

Meet Carol, strong in Bounceback...

"I've been through some real ups and downs in my life, but I've always managed to use them to come out fighting. I remember once that I applied for a job that I thought was made for me — I even knew the people involved and spoke to them and got the nod that I was the person they were looking for. But then they gave it to someone else. I was devastated, but in no time at all I'd turned around that disappointment into a drive to do even better. 'I'll show you' I thought — and ever since then, I have — I've done better than I could ever imagined, and it feels great when I look back at them and think 'You could have had this' but instead, I know I have done it for myself."

Bounceback Hall of Fame...

- **Lance Armstrong** — American athlete and winner of a record 7 Tour de France cycle races; diagnosed with cancer and surgically treated for brain tumours, but still returned to win an additional five Tour de France races.

- **Paula Radcliffe** — British long distance runner and holder of several world records despite numerous injuries and comebacks.

- **Wilma Rudolph** — First US woman to win three Olympic gold medals in track and field events, doing so despite overcoming infantile paralysis as a result of childhood polio.

Bounceback in Relationships — What Works and What to Watch Out For...

You are likely to look at relationships as a growth experience. You tend to have long-term relationships because you are confident that you can weather short-term conflict and problems. If something doesn't work out as you want in a relationship, you'll bounce back and try again.

Bounceback at Work — Occupations Where You Could Find a Fit...

- Author;
- Firefighter;
- Police officer;
- Social worker;
- Stockbroker.

Bounceback at Play — Leisure Suggestions You Might Enjoy...

- Boxing;
- Chess;
- Golf;
- Triathlon;
- Rock climbing.

But Don't Take It Too Far...Bounceback Overplayed...

Don't become a struggle-seeker, relying on your Bounceback to recover! Your strength in responding positively to setbacks and negative experiences can, if overplayed, lead you to continually put yourself in, or be put in, situations that require you to recover from disappointments or turn things around. Create time to recover and recuperate from challenges. Crucially, set aside time to learn from these experiences, rather than moving straight from one to the next.

Catalyst

People strong in Catalyst motivate and inspire others to make things happen.

If You Have a Strength in Catalyst...

You are the type of person who loves to mobilise and inspire other people to take part in a range of activities and projects. You especially enjoy getting new projects off the ground and putting ideas into action by involving others. You get people excited about new projects and motivate them to work on things that otherwise they might never have done.

The Catalyst Catchphrase...

"Together we can do it!"

Meet Thomas, strong in Catalyst...

"I've just recently taken forward a whole new approach to recruitment. For me this was just something that was too important to pass by — it was just going to make a big difference to the way we did things. I had to get other people on board with my ideas, so I just went for it. I just love getting that injection of input from somebody that I trust and respect, knowing myself that this is the way forward, this is the next big thing and what we as a business should be working on. And then to go and get other people excited about it, and embrace it, and hold onto it, and see it though. That's what I love to do."

Catalyst Hall of Fame...

- **Mohandas (Mahatma) Gandhi** — Political and spiritual leader of India during the Indian independence movement; pioneered *satyagraha* (civil disobedience) founded upon *ahimsa* (non-violence) and led India to independence, inspiring movements for civil rights and freedom across the world.

- **Whitney Houston** — American recording artist who is credited with opening up opportunities for other female black artists through her appearances on music television and radio.

- **Martin Luther King, Jr.** – African-American clergyman, activist and civil rights leader; inspired public consciousness of the civil rights movement through his famous "I Have a Dream" speech.

Catalyst in Relationships – What Works and What to Watch Out For...

You tend to have a utilitarian view of relationships. You get excited by inspiring others and get the greatest charge out of knowing that your relationship are in the service of accomplishing an objective. Be careful that you don't lose sight of the intrinsic value of your relationships – that they are good in and of themselves – rather than just as a means for you to get things done.

Catalyst at Work – Occupations Where You Could Find a Fit...

- Community worker;
- Educator;
- Event promoter;
- Political activist;
- Politician.

Catalyst at Play – Leisure Suggestions You Might Enjoy...

- Charity work;
- Coaching;
- Home theatre groups;
- Organising children's sports leagues;
- Playing team sports.

But Don't Take It Too Far...Catalyst Overplayed...

Don't lose your focus or spread yourself too thin! Your strength in motivating and inspiring others to make things happen and mobilising people to get involved can, if overplayed, result in you abandoning your responsibilities to others. Limit the number of projects you initiate and commit time and effort to making these successful before moving on.

Centred

People strong in Centred have an inner composure and self-assurance, whatever the situation.

If You Have a Strength in Centred...

You feel as though you look out at the world with confidence, being grounded in the solid foundation of your sense of self, your deep knowledge of who and what you are. You love to feel the natural sense of self-assurance that you maintain almost effortlessly in any situation. Whatever challenges life throws at you, your sense of poise and composure is never shaken. Others respect and admire you for this. You feel totally — and naturally — at ease with yourself at all times and in all situations.

The Centred Catchphrase...

"Calm above all things."

Meet Zoe, strong in Centred...

"People ask me to do things all the time. I think I get asked because they know that I will do them properly and not get into a flap when faced by something different or new. Only the other day I got asked by a friend of my daughter to help backstage at the local amateur dramatic association's latest performance of *Carousel*. It was quite demanding, calling different people at various times and making sure that all were on stage when they should have been. I think people ask me because they feel confident that I won't panic."

Centred Hall of Fame...

- **HH Dalai Lama** — The spiritual leader of the Tibetan people; Nobel Peace Prize recipient in recognition of his leadership of the non-violent struggle for the liberation of Tibet.

- **Vera Lynn** — English singer who became known as "the Forces' sweetheart" during the Second World War, when her song "We'll Meet Again" became emblematic of the era.

- **C. B. "Sully" Sullenberger** — Pilot who landed US Airways Flight 1549 in the Hudson River (2009) following a collision with a flock of geese that destroyed both engines of the plane.

Centred in Relationships — What Works and What to Watch Out For...

People know you as someone who is "easy to get along with." You are hard to ruffle and you tend not to stoop too low in arguments. People see you as dependable, somebody they can trust. For all of these reasons, people will consider you a rock in relationships.

Centred at Work — Occupations Where You Could Find a Fit...

- Airline pilot;
- Diplomat;
- Funeral director;
- Public relations officer;
- Surgeon.

Centred at Play — Leisure Suggestions You Might Enjoy...

- Chess;
- Hiking;
- Meditation;
- Tea tasting;
- Yoga.

But Don't Take It Too Far...Centred Overplayed...

Don't forget to relax! Your strength in projecting a sense of assurance and composure whatever the situation can, if overplayed, convey a lack of enthusiasm or an unwillingness to be move to action. Know when to moderate your calmness and self-assurance with enthusiasm and spontaneity, recognising that sometimes it's better to reveal your feelings.

Change
Agent

People strong in Change Agent are constantly involved with change, advocating for change and making it happen.

If You Have a Strength in Change Agent...

Change energises you. You are able to see the real benefits of change and always love to be involved with and to bring about change in some way or another. You often become an advocate for new developments and relish any opportunity to implement change. Your enthusiasm for change enthuses others, who may otherwise have been more reluctant about the change.

The Change Agent Catchphrase...

"Change is the only constant."

Meet Sally, strong in Change Agent...

"The primary thing which excites me is that the UK market is a free market. The significant thing that I am really giddy about is that it is a free market and I can pretty much do what I want to, to pricing the product, setting up new distribution, exploiting the opportunities that are there. The only thing that is holding us back is how fast can we implement change and how we make sure we bring the rest of the organisation with us, it's a really exciting time and one that I love being involved in. The basic idea is that you can help to evolve and change the market, we are going to be doing things that nobody else in the market place is going to be doing. So we will be highly innovative and that will hopefully play out in growth and profitability. My biggest role — and the thing I love doing — is to identify the changes we need to make and then get the buy-in we need to make them happen. Bring it on, I say."

Change Agent Hall of Fame...

- **Mikhail Gorbachev** — Former leader of the Soviet Union; best known for his dramatic policy reforms, including *perestroika* (restructuring) and *glasnost* (openness), and his ability to work with non-communist heads of state.
- **Germaine Greer** — Author of *The Female Eunuch*, widely regarded as being one of the most influential feminist voices of the 20th century.
- **Beverly Naidoo** — South African children's author who writes about her experiences under the apartheid regime and was arrested for her activities as part of the resistance movement in South Africa.

Change Agent in Relationships — What Works and What to Watch Out For...

You may have a tendency to focus more on your mission for what you want to change than on those around you. Although you appreciate help and support, remember to express it to those who are important to you. Be careful, as well, that your Change Agent doesn't overtake you in relationships, meaning that you always want to change the people around you as well.

Change Agent at Work — Occupations Where You Could Find a Fit...

- Change consultant;
- Marketing executive;
- Policymaker;
- Politician;
- Social activist.

Change Agent at Play — Leisure Suggestions You Might Enjoy...

- Children's advocacy;
- Civic or local government positions;
- Environmental activism;
- Mentoring;
- Volunteering.

But Don't Take It Too Far...Change Agent Overplayed...

Avoid change for the sake of change! Your strength in embracing change and involving yourself actively in the process of change can, if overplayed, lead to instability and uncertainty for other people. Learn when change is necessary, as well as when it isn't.

Compassion

People strong in Compassion really care about others, doing all they can to help.

If You Have a Strength in Compassion...

You have an open heart and care about all the people around you. You want the best for everyone and offer sympathy and support to others, especially in times of suffering. When people are unhappy, you look for the right thing to say and take action to help people in whatever way you can.

The Compassion Catchphrase...

"I feel your pain..."

Meet John, strong in Compassion...

"I care deeply that the people working for me are okay and I have done the 'Uncle John' bit with a number of people a lot over the years and still do. People come to me because they know that I care. There was someone who I believed was being bullied in the work place. I felt deeply for him and put my own head on the block to sort it out. I'm glad I did because he is now ok and I get a huge sense of satisfaction that, because I cared, there is now a repaired human individual."

Compassion Hall of Fame...

- **Diana, Princess of Wales** — The first wife of Prince Charles, the Prince of Wales; known for her charitable work, particularly concerning AIDS awareness and landmines.

- **Oskar Schindler** — German industrialist who is credited with saving 1,200 Jews during the Holocaust, by employing them in his enamelware and munitions factories.

- **Mary Seacole** — Jamaican-born British nurse who applied to the War Office to serve in the Crimean War as a nurse, but was turned down; unperturbed, she borrowed the money to make the 4,000 mile journey herself, treating the wounded from both sides while under fire.

Compassion in Relationships — What Works and What to Watch Out For...

You tend to have a deep connection with others and a care-taking nature. Be careful to take the time to take care of yourself as well, so that others do not take too much from you, leaving you feeling that you are overspent and in need of other people's compassion.

Compassion at Work — Occupations Where You Could Find a Fit...

- Aid worker;
- Bereavement counsellor;
- Nurse;
- Palliative care worker;
- Veterinary surgeon.

Compassion at Play — Leisure Suggestions You Might Enjoy...

- Animal shelter volunteer;
- Community advocacy;
- Nursing home volunteer;
- Paralympics volunteer;
- Pets.

But Don't Take It Too Far...Compassion Overplayed...

Be careful not to suffocate people with your compassion! Your strength in reaching out to people when they are unhappy or are suffering can, if overplayed, be misplaced or misguided. Know when compassion is not required or may not be helpful. Balance your compassion with a capacity for practical support and advice as well.

Competitive

People strong in Competitive are constantly competing to win.

If You Have a Strength in Competitive...

You are highly motivated by competing against others. Measuring your abilities relative to others is how you gauge your progress and success. You love to make everything into a contest. You want to perform quicker and better than everyone at everything you do. For you, winning is the only option. You feel great when you are first, but tend to take it hard when you lose — in fact, for you, losing hurts.

The Competitive Catchphrase...

"I play to win."

Meet Rachel, strong in Competitive ...

"I'm a very competitive person. It sounds a cliché to say, but when you wake up in the morning one of the first things that enters my head is that I want to be the best at what I do. When I get into the office and start looking at stuff, I do think about winning ...I want to beat these guys, and I think about how I am going to do it. Every week or two you need a win that you can celebrate. I hate to say that I have to have that, but I probably do."

Competitive Hall of Fame...

- **Muhammad Ali** — Retired American boxer and three-time World Heavyweight Champion; would often provoke opponents or celebrate victories with his claim that "I am the greatest".

- **Billie Jean King** — American tennis player and winner of 12 Grand Slam women's singles titles, 16 Grand Slam women's doubles titles, and 11 Grand Slam mixed doubles titles.

- **Michael Phelps** — Winner of a record 8 Olympic Gold Medals in the Beijing Olympics 2008.

Competitive in Relationships — What Works and What to Watch Out For...

You relate to others through competition, friendly or otherwise. You may have a tendency to push others or to tease. You should remember that although some people will find it endearing, others do not have the same tolerance for competition that you do.

Competitive at Work — Occupations Where You Could Find a Fit...

- Chef;
- Consultant;
- Fundraiser;
- PR agent;
- Salesperson.

Competitive at Play — Leisure Suggestions You Might Enjoy...

- Backgammon/poker;
- Bowling;
- Competitive sports;
- Organised gaming leagues;
- Video games.

But Don't Take It Too Far...Competitive Overplayed...

Know when competition is unhealthy! Your strength in being competitive and measuring your progress and success against others can, if overplayed, impact negatively on your health, well-being and relationships. Know when competing will be detrimental to the other things that are important in your life.

Connector

People strong in Connector make connections between people, instinctively making links and introductions.

If You Have a Strength in Connector...

Whatever situation you find yourself in, you always love making connections between the people that you meet. You notice when people have shared interests or something in common and you instinctively make links between them, thinking about the ways you can effectively bring people together for their mutual benefit.

The Connector Catchphrase...

"Let me introduce you to..."

Meet Emma, strong in Connector...

"I love bringing the right people together so that everyone has a really good time. I spend a lot of time thinking about who comes to the events that I arrange. I like to ensure that there are people there who have something in common with each other. The last event that I arranged was a networking event at the local race track. We had people coming from all over the country and from a variety of different businesses so on the face of it there was little in common. But I knew that one business had just taken a huge step in introducing a new concept to their business and another was thinking along similar lines but was unsure, so I made sure that they met and had the chance to talk about things. I like nothing better than to introduce different people to each other who I know share some sort of common bond, spend a short time with them, and then I move on to make further introductions. I get a huge buzz from that."

Connector Hall of Fame...

- **Julie and Steve Pankhurst** — Founders of online social network site Friends Reunited, which achieved 15 million members within five years of its launch.

- **Therese Prentice** — Social networking and network marketing specialist, through the website socialnetworkingqueen.com
- **Klaus Schwab** — Founder of the annual business and political gathering, the World Economic Forum, and subsequently the Schwab Foundation for Social Entrepreneurship.

Connector in Relationships — What Works and What to Watch Out For...

You are a very social person and want the people you know to know one another. You like to watch others make and maintain connections. You get a charge out of new meetings and gatherings, and others will often recognise you as the social glue that brings people together.

Connector at Work — Occupations Where You Could Find a Fit...

- Dating agent;
- Estate agent;
- Event organiser;
- Recruitment consultant;
- Volunteer co-ordinator.

Connector at Play — Leisure Suggestions You Might Enjoy...

- Amateur radio;
- Civic or business clubs;
- Community volunteer co-ordinator;
- Entertaining and hosting;
- Social networking.

But Don't Take It Too Far...Connector Overplayed...

Don't forget to connect yourself! Your strength in making connections between people and bringing them together can, if overplayed, become a barrier to you connecting with individuals yourself, in the moment. Develop, and if necessary delay your capacity to connect others until you have got to know the person to whom you are talking.

Counterpoint

People strong in Counterpoint always bring a different viewpoint to others — whatever the situation or context.

If You Have a Strength in Counterpoint...

You love to bring an alternative perspective to any situation. You seem to see things differently from others, and can present a range of options, possibilities and alternatives for any scenario. As a result, you will often bring things into the discussion that other people have missed.

The Counterpoint Catchphrase...

"We could look at things this way..."

Meet George, strong in Counterpoint...

"We were sitting in a meeting the other day, discussing how we should spend a small award that had been allocated to us. The main ideas on the table were to concentrate on the academic side of things and the usual things such as books and learning resources were mentioned. I sat back for a bit and then said that we had always spent money on those, and as this was a special pot of money, that it could be spent on other things such as the music or the drama departments. I put forward different ideas which I think were well received by most. I like to do that — to bounce different ideas around and get people to think about things in different ways."

Counterpoint Hall of Fame...

- **Rachel Carson** — American marine biologist and nature writer, whose book *Silent Spring* (1962) led to a reversal in US pesticide policy, and massive popular interest in environmental concerns, ultimately prompting the establishment of the Environmental Protection Agency.

- **Nassim Nicholas Taleb** — Author of *The Black Swan*, in which he argues that one-off, unpredictable events can lead to massive consequences — in contrast to almost all other economic theories.

- **Vivienne Westwood** – British fashion designer who is considered instrumental in bringing punk and new wave fashions into the mainstream; three-time winner of the British Fashion Designer of the Year Award and a Dame of the British Empire.

Counterpoint in Relationships – What Works and What to Watch Out For...

You play "devil's advocate" and don't mind a little arguing or conflict in your relationships. Remember, not everyone shares your tolerance for conflict, so use this gift wisely. Sometimes, people might need a rest from your ability always to introduce another perspective.

Counterpoint at Work – Occupations Where You Could Find a Fit...

- Barrister;
- Comedian;
- Editor;
- Film maker;
- Research scientist.

Counterpoint at Play – Leisure Suggestions You Might Enjoy...

- Blogging;
- Debating;
- Handwriting analysis;
- Toastmaster/toastmistress;
- Writing letters to the editor.

But Don't Take It Too Far...Counterpoint Overplayed...

Know when not to be different! Your strength in always bringing things into a discussion that others have missed, or offering a different viewpoint to others can, if overplayed, come across as annoying and obstructive. Be prepared, sometimes, to join the majority rather than sticking resolutely in your minority of one.

Courage

People strong in Courage overcome their fears and do what they want to do in spite of them.

If You Have a Strength in Courage...

While you may well feel afraid, your Courage means that you are always able to face down and overcome your fears. You get a buzz from participating in activities that make you nervous or scared, never letting your fear get in the way of what you want to do.

The Courage Catchphrase...

"Feel the fear and do it anyway..."

Meet Helen, strong in Courage...

"I do like to travel — I want to see and experience all there is to see and do. There is just one slight drawback though — I am terrified of flying and of snakes, terrified of enclosed spaces and of heights, and also get pretty nervous about getting sick from food and water when I travel. So as you can see, getting places and sometimes even being there is a bit scary for me. Somehow though, I do it, I just seem to find the strength from within to do those things that scare me."

Courage Hall of Fame...

- **Douglas Bader** — Royal Air Force fighter ace who fought in the Second World War despite previously having lost both his legs.

- **Aung San Suu Kyi** — Nobel Peace Prize recipient and peace activist; best known for speaking out against the military junta in Myanmar.

- **Harriet Tubman** — The first woman to lead an armed expedition in the American Civil War; she had previously helped slaves to escape using the network of activists and safe houses known as the Underground Railroad.

Courage in Relationships — What Works and What to Watch Out For...

You are likely to "be yourself" even if this means taking risks in relationships or sticking up for unpopular people or ideas. Be mindful not to put yourself — or others in your relationships — into situations of undue risk. Equally, your courage will make you a loyal friend and somebody on whom people feel that they can depend.

Courage at Work — Occupations Where You Could Find a Fit...

- Court advocate;
- Firefighter;
- Intelligence officer;
- Lifeguard;
- Stunt person.

Courage at Play — Leisure Suggestions You Might Enjoy...

- Extreme sports;
- Hot air ballooning;
- Motorcycling;
- Police volunteer;
- Potholing/caving.

But Don't Take It Too Far...Courage Overplayed...

Don't become a fear-facing addict! Your strength in doing what you want to do in spite of your fears can, if overplayed, lead you to become addicted to seeking out fear-raising experiences. Create moments of calm — don't push yourself continually to face up to one fear after another.

Creativity

People strong in Creativity strive to produce work that is new and original, creating and combining things in novel and imaginative ways.

If You Have a Strength in Creativity...

Creativity is at your core. You love to be coming up with or combining new ideas, images, colours, tastes or concepts. You thrive on breaking new ground, trying things that have not been tried before, linking things in novel and imaginative ways and creating something from nothing.

The Creativity Catchphrase...

"I wonder what would happen if..."

Meet Helen, strong in Creativity...

"I make doing the housework a pleasure because I am always thinking of ways that I can arrange things in a different way. It takes the monotony out of things although I'm not so sure that I always get all the housework done! The other day I spotted a table that was just lying there doing nothing, so I worked my magic on it and now it is the focal point of the room. I also like to cook and I do this in a very imaginative way. I just love combining different ingredients together in unusual ways, mixing different tastes, colours and textures. My family and friends say that they love coming around to eat, because they are always in for a surprise, something different."

Creativity Hall of Fame...

- **Tracey Emin** — One of the group known as the Young British Artists; Turner Prize nominee and Royal Academician of the Royal Academy of Arts in London; renowned for her controversial art work.

- **Steve Jobs** — Founder of Apple Inc., the producers of the iPod, iPhone, Mac and other innovative brands, renowned for their design and aesthetic appeal.

- **Beatrix Potter** – Author and illustrator of 23 children's books featuring animal characters, the most famous of which is probably *The Tale of Peter Rabbit*.

Creativity in Relationships – What Works and What to Watch Out For...

You are the type of person who enjoys play, banter and a fresh perspective in your relationships. You like surprises and enjoy finding new ways of expressing your feelings for others. This can mean that people think you are really fun to be around – just so long as you don't take your creativity too far!

Creativity at Work – Occupations Where You Could Find a Fit...

- Chef;
- Designer;
- Interior decorator;
- Landscape gardener;
- Musician.

Creativity at Play – Leisure Suggestions You Might Enjoy...

- Macramé;
- Musical composition;
- Painting;
- Web design;
- Woodworking.

But Don't Take It Too Far...Creativity Overplayed...

Don't just be a dreamer! Your strength in coming up with new things and different ways of doing things, producing work that is new and original can, if overplayed, limit the extent to which you achieve anything concrete. Learn to balance your creativity with a capacity to be planful and to deliver, in order to bring your new and original ideas to fruition.

Curiosity

People strong in Curiosity are interested in everything, constantly seeking out new information and learning more.

If You Have a Strength in Curiosity...

You are interested in everything. Being very open to new ideas, you constantly seek out new information. You get excited when you discover new topics to study. You're unlikely to let fascinating points, no matter how minor, pass you by — without trying to find out more about them. You love to ask questions, do follow-up reading, or make your own enquiries to learn more about the topics you come across from day to day.

The Curiosity Catchphrase...

"Tell me more...What?...Why?...When did that happen?..."

Meet Georgie, strong in Curiosity...

"I've always been fascinated by the way that people learn. The children in my class are all different, with some learning by 'doing stuff' and others by talking about things and so on. I want to get the best I can from the children who come to me, so I am always on the lookout for articles in papers and magazines which debate different learning styles. I talk to different teachers and parents about their experiences. It's a fascinating subject and I just can't get enough of it. In fact, it's the same for so many things — I just find so much so interesting!"

Curiosity Hall of Fame...

- **Tycho Brahe** — 16th century Danish astronomer who carefully observed the night sky and a number of unusual astronomic phenomena such as a supernova.

- **Marie Curie** — Twice Nobel Prize recipient in Physics and Chemistry for her discovery of elements and research on radiation.

• **Charles Darwin** — Leading naturalist credited with the discovery of the theory of evolution, published in *The Origin of the Species*.

Curiosity in Relationships — What Works and What to Watch Out For...

You are socially inquisitive by nature. You can be a good listener and are attracted to interesting personal stories and new ideas. You ask many questions and can have a tendency to want to explore people and their experiences continually, being especially interested in anything that is novel or unusual for you. Be careful not to lose interest in people once your curiosity has been satisfied about them — people can be eternal mysteries!

Curiosity at Work — Occupations Where You Could Find a Fit...

• Archaeologist;
• Fraud investigator;
• Historian;
• Market researcher;
• Psychologist.

Curiosity at Play — Leisure Suggestions You Might Enjoy...

• Genealogy;
• Internet browsing;
• Metal detecting;
• Museum visiting;
• Reading.

But Don't Take It Too Far...Curiosity Overplayed...

Don't forget to act on your ideas! Your strength in seeking out new information and your interest in new ideas can, if overplayed, impact negatively on your ability to get things done. It may also irritate or overwhelm people if you are constantly asking questions. Not everyone has the same appetite for learning as you do. Learn to spot when you need to move from reflecting and questioning and into planning and action.

Detail

People strong in Detail naturally focus on the small things that others easily miss, ensuring that everything is accurate and error-free.

If You Have a Strength in Detail...

You have a natural ability to focus on the smallest detail. You quickly and easily spot inaccuracies, inconsistencies and mistakes. Errors seem to jump out at you and you get a real buzz from being able to correct them. You get a great sense of satisfaction when you are able to check that details are accurate and complete. Paying attention to detail is very important to you — you would never submit anything yourself that contained a mistake.

The Detail Catchphrase...

"It's important to get things just right..."

Meet Gerald, strong in Detail...

"I'm renowned for noticing the smallest detail. I was listening to someone give a presentation the other day and as soon as the slides were put up I noticed that there was a spelling mistake on one of the slides. Nobody else seemed to notice it and I must admit that the writing on the slide was very tiny, but to me I just couldn't help but notice. I had to tell everyone, so that hopefully that slide will get altered for the next time. It irritates me that people don't tend to notice these things. I make sure that everything I do is properly finished off and that there are no mistakes. Every email that I send, I check through to make sure that the spelling and grammar are right."

Detail Hall of Fame...

- **Zaha Hadid** — British Iraqi architect who has won many international competitions with her theoretically influential and groundbreaking architectural designs.

- **James Murray** — Editor-in-Chief of the magnificent Oxford English Dictionary.

- **Arlene Phillips** — English choreographer of numerous West End and Broadway musicals; a judge on BBC One's *Strictly Come Dancing* from 2004–2008.

Detail in Relationships — What Works and What to Watch Out For...

You keep track of the little things— birthdays, what was said, the fine points of how a person looks. You are observant with your friends and other people tend to appreciate your attention to detail. Ensure though that you find time to relax in relationships — you'll enjoy them even more if you do!

Detail at Work — Occupations Where You Could Find a Fit...

- Cartographer;
- Jeweller;
- Pattern cutter;
- Pharmacist;
- Proofreader/copy editor.

Detail at Play — Leisure Suggestions You Might Enjoy...

- Airplane modelling;
- Archaeology;
- Beadwork;
- Needlepoint;
- Pyrotechnics.

But Don't Take It Too Far...Detail Overplayed...

Know when to settle for "good enough". Your strength in focusing on detail, noticing and correcting errors can, if overplayed, hinder progress inappropriately. Spot when a situation demands you to focus less on detail, for example, when a piece of work needs to be achieved urgently, or when 100% is just not necessary. Learn how to dial your detail strength up or down as the situation requires.

Drive

People strong in Drive are self-motivated and push themselves hard to achieve what they want out of life.

If You Have a Strength in Drive...

You are extremely self-motivated with an inner drive and motivation that pushes you to achieve more. You never need to be told what to do next. As soon as you complete one task, you move on to the next. You love to set your own goals and targets — often higher than those that others may have set for you.

The Drive Catchphrase...

"Tick. What's next?"

Meet Philip, strong in Drive...

"I always have to be busy, the only thing that stops me from working is when I am ill and being ill is a great frustration to me. I have a to-do list which I set for myself every morning. I love looking at it, rewriting it, and crossing things off. I just love crossing things off, some of the things that I cross off can be quite trivial and sometimes I think that I just put them on so that I can just cross them off. I always give myself work to do and if I manage to complete all that I have set myself at the beginning of the day, then I feel that I have had a good day, that I have achieved something."

Drive Hall of Fame...

- **Alexander the Great** — Macedonian king who conquered 90% of the known world by the age of 32 years, campaigning as far as modern India and Pakistan before having to turn back because of a near-mutiny by his troops.

- **Amelia Earhardt** — American aviator; first woman to fly solo across the Atlantic Ocean, for which she was awarded the Distinguished Flying Cross.

- **Margaret Thatcher** — Former leader of the Conservative Party and first female British Prime Minister, the only woman to have held either post.

Drive in Relationships — What Works and What to Watch Out For...

You are likely to be focused on what you achieve by spending time on your relationships. Recognise that sometimes it's okay just to relax and not worry about what you are getting done. Success is sometimes achieved by doing less, so learn to spot the signs and what this means for your relationships and the people around you.

Drive at Work — Occupations Where You Could Find a Fit...

- Business manager;
- Entrepreneur;
- Professional services worker;
- Salesperson;
- Teacher.

Drive at Play — Leisure Suggestions You Might Enjoy...

- Marathon running;
- Martial arts;
- Parachuting;
- Water polo;
- Windsurfing.

But Don't Take It Too Far...Drive Overplayed...

Know when to relax! Your strength in pushing yourself hard to achieve what you want out of life can, if overplayed, impact negatively on your health, well-being, and relationships. Strive for a balance that meets not just your desire to achieve things, but also your wider life needs and interests.

Efficacy

People strong in Efficacy are very confident in their own abilities, having a sure belief that they can achieve their goals.

If You Have a Strength in Efficacy...

You are very confident and self-assured, with an unwavering belief in your own strengths and abilities. With this self-confidence, you always believe that you can achieve the goals towards which you are working. You have a "can do" attitude to life, believing that almost anything is within your reach if you set your mind to it and work hard to achieve it. This self-belief shines through every day and instils a confidence in the people around you.

The Efficacy Catchphrase...

"Yes, I can..."

Meet David, strong in Efficacy...

"I know that I am good at selling to people. People have told me — and my sales figures are there as evidence. It doesn't seem to matter what it is that I am selling, I know that when I go into the sales room, people are going to buy from me. I think if you start to let negativity creep in, then that is where you are going to fail. The other day, my colleague came down and said that she was getting nowhere fast with some clients, and she believed that they were going to walk out of the door. She was very down because what we had done for these clients was top notch. I asked if I could take over and give it a try. I did — and I completely turned them around. The thing is — I knew that I would, I knew that we had something good to offer, and I think it is that confidence that they picked up on."

Efficacy Hall of Fame...

- **Joan of Arc** — National heroine of France and a Catholic saint; led the French Army to several important victories as a teenager during the Hundred Years War, but was ultimately burned at the stake at the age of just 19 years.

- **Lee Kuan Yew** — Founder of modern Singapore; credited with building the jungle island into an Asian financial capital.

- **Oprah Winfrey** — American billionaire and television personality; known for her leading talk show, *The Oprah Winfrey Show*, her book club and magazines, and other merchandising of the Oprah Winfrey brand that she created from scratch.

Efficacy in Relationships — What Works and What to Watch Out For...

You believe you can achieve almost anything you set your mind to, and naturally expect others to feel the same about themselves. Recognise that not everyone shares this self-confidence, and allow people to hold back when they feel more comfortable doing so. Equally, keep an eye on how you can use your own sense of efficacy to help others through your relationships with them.

Efficacy at Work — Occupations Where You Could Find a Fit...

- Author;
- Consultant;
- Entrepreneur;
- Financial advisor;
- Tradesperson.

Efficacy at Play — Leisure Suggestions You Might Enjoy...

- Climbing;
- Endurance sports;
- Golf;
- Horse riding;
- Mentoring.

But Don't Take It Too Far...Efficacy Overplayed...

Don't be arrogant! Your strength in believing that you can achieve things, together with your confidence and self-assurance about your own abilities can, if overplayed, be judged by others as arrogant. Learn to monitor how you come across to others, and balance your confidence with a degree of humility where appropriate.

Emotional Awareness

People strong in Emotional Awareness are acutely aware of the emotions and feelings of others.

If You Have a Strength in Emotional Awareness...

You are an excellent judge of people's emotions and feelings. You want to know how people are feeling and have a keen eye and an intuitive ear, which helps you pick up on subtle clues and messages that people give out. You receive these messages and quickly and accurately interpret them so that people's emotions are very clear to you.

The Emotional Awareness Catchphrase...

"I know how you feel..."

Meet Gloria, strong in Emotional Awareness...

"I seem to be able to notice if somebody is not happy within the team or feeling slightly stressed or pressurised. For instance, yesterday, I noticed that one of the people in my team seemed not to be herself. So when I got the chance I asked if she was ok. It was like the floodgates were opened and a whole raft of issues came out, some personal ones, some related to work, and so we talked it through. I was able to provide support and let her know that that I was there for her. It's not something that I just do at work, I seem to do it all the time — even with people that I don't really know very well. I just seem to have this emotional barometer, which I have learned to take notice of and respect."

Emotional Awareness Hall of Fame...

- **Kiran Desai** — Man Booker Prize-winning novelist for her novel *The Inheritance of Loss*, which focused on the emotional experiences of its protagonists.

- **Karen Horney** — German psychologist and psychotherapist who developed a theory of neurosis as a way of coping when the human striving for self-realisation was being thwarted; best known for her book *Neurosis and Human Growth* (1950).
- **Robert Smith** — Lead singer, guitarist and songwriter for British rock group The Cure; renowned for his ability to convey the full range of emotions through his music and lyrics, from deep, dark introspection through to quirky, upbeat pop.

Emotional Awareness in Relationships — What Works and What to Watch Out For...

You have an easy time connecting with others and are sensitive even to minor emotional cues. Not everyone is as savvy as you in the language of emotion, however, and may not be as comfortable as you are in identifying or talking about feelings. Give people their own space and allow them their own emotional preferences.

Emotional Awareness at Work — Occupations Where You Could Find a Fit...

- Child care worker;
- Counsellor;
- Group facilitator;
- Masseur/masseuse;
- Mediator.

Emotional Awareness at Play — Leisure Suggestions You Might Enjoy...

- Child advocacy;
- Entertaining/hosting;
- Men's group/women's group;
- Nursing home volunteer;
- Poker.

But Don't Take It Too Far...Emotional Awareness Overplayed...

Don't be too sensitive! Your strength in picking up on subtle clues and messages can, if overplayed, stifle your natural interaction with others. You may have a tendency to comment on other people's emotions, which could leave them self-conscious or rob situations of their spontaneous nature. Know when to take people just as they are.

Empathic Connection

People strong in Empathic Connection feel connected to others through their ability to sense and understand what other people are feeling.

If You Have a Strength in Empathic Connection...

You have a natural connection with other people, where you are very finely tuned in to other people and can feel what they are feeling. You love to put yourself "in another person's shoes", to experience the same emotions they are experiencing. You share their joy, their pain, their frustration and their elation. Your Empathic Connection means that you are always able to see things from another person's point of view, to understand them all the better for doing so.

The Empathic Connection Catchphrase...

"I feel it too..."

Meet Esther, strong in Empathic Connection...

"People ring me up and sometimes you could just cry with some of the stories that they tell you. One particular chap and his girlfriend had had a particular horrendous experience where they had crashed the car down an embankment whilst he was letting her have a 'quick practice' at driving in a car park. It involved the police, the ambulance and the fire brigade and as they weren't insured was going to cost an awful lot. I really felt for them, I have teenage children myself and I could just imagine what they were going through. I gave that case a lot of my time and attention, it just felt right to do so."

Empathic Connection Hall of Fame...

- **Shahruk Khan** — Indian Bollywood actor and winner of 13 Filmfare Awards; renowned for his ability to connect with his audience.
- **Esther Rantzen** — Television presenter and founder of the child protection charity, ChildLine.

- **Carl Rogers** — Influential American psychologist who was one of the founders of humanistic psychology; developed the person-centred approach and client-centred therapy.

Empathic Connection in Relationships — What Works and What to Watch Out For...

You have a unique ability to put yourself in the positions of others. You are able to connect easily with others and express concern for people in need. Just be careful that you don't allow yourself to be overwhelmed by the emotions of the people around you, ensuring that you use your Empathic Connection to look after yourself and your own emotional needs as well.

Empathic Connection at Work — Occupations Where You Could Find a Fit...

- Child care worker;
- Counsellor;
- Nurse;
- Priest;
- Social worker.

Empathic Connection at Play — Leisure Suggestions You Might Enjoy...

- Animal rescue;
- Crisis volunteer;
- Reading novels;
- Telephone counsellor;
- Theatre.

But Don't Take It Too Far...Empathic Connection Overplayed...

Protect your emotional state! Your strength in sensing what other people are feeling and tuning in to what other people are thinking can, if overplayed, lead you to become overwhelmed by other people's distress. Learn to distance yourself emotionally when you need to do so. Protect your own emotional well-being at the same time as you connect with the emotions of others.

Enabler

People strong in Enabler create the conditions for people to grow and develop for themselves.

If You Have a Strength in Enabler...

You enjoy developing people so that they can do things for themselves. At the same time as providing support and encouragement, you give people tasks and challenges that you know will stretch them, pushing them out of their comfort zone in ways that will help them to grow and develop.

The Enabler Catchphrase...

"You can do it..."

Meet Victor, strong in Enabler...

"I absolutely want people to become better at what they do. That gives me great satisfaction. I had a secretary who wanted to do her IPD qualifications and the big boss said absolutely no, because what would probably happen is that she would become qualified and then leave. My response was that she would leave anyway if we didn't. I had already seen her potential by asking her to do more and more stretching jobs for me, so I knew she could do it. So she did her IPD qualification, and then from being a secretary, she got her first HR manager job under me. She worked with me for a number of years and has now progressed to be the HR manager of a TV company — which is just fantastic for her."

Enabler Hall of Fame...

- **Brian Clough** — Former manager of Nottingham Forest Football Club, twice consecutive winners of the European Cup in 1979 and 1980, despite having been promoted from the old Second Division only two years before.

- **Maria Montessori** — Founder of the Montessori system of schools which places the capabilities and interests of the child as central, treating them as competent beings capable of making their own decisions.

- **Anthony Robbins** — American self-improvement guru and best-selling author who has helped millions to improve their lives; best known for his book *Awaken the Giant Within*.

Enabler in Relationships — What Works and What to Watch Out For...

You like to bring out the best in others. You are a supportive and, at times, challenging friend and colleague. Make sure the people around you want your help before you offer it. Your desire to help others to grow and develop can be misdirected if you end up pushing people further than they are ready to go — enjoy relationships for what they are sometimes, rather than what they could become.

Enabler at Work — Occupations Where You Could Find a Fit...

- Coach;
- Community worker;
- Occupational therapist;
- Teacher;
- Youth worker.

Enabler at Play — Leisure Suggestions You Might Enjoy...

- Coaching;
- Community organising;
- Mentoring;
- Reading to children;
- Youth work volunteer.

But Don't Take It Too Far...Enabler Overplayed...

Don't push too far or too fast! Your strength in creating the conditions for people to grow and develop, helping them become better equipped for future challenges, can, if overplayed, be misdirected. Spot when you are pushing someone too far out of their comfort zone, or when they need to take shelter from being challenged. Let people find their own level and pace.

Equality

People strong in Equality ensure that everyone is treated equally.

If You Have a Strength in Equality...

Being fair and equitable is at the heart of who you are. You consider everyone to be your equal and give great attention to issues of fairness and equality. You love to make sure that all people are treated equally and that your own actions and decisions are as fair and equitable as possible.

The Equality Catchphrase...

"Everybody is equal."

Meet Richard, strong in Equality...

"I absolutely believe that everyone should be treated fairly and equally. Whatever I am doing, I strive to get a fair outcome for all. I love to create win-win situations where everyone is treated fairly and with respect. I hate the short-sighted views that some people adopt when they win in certain situations but which mean that someone out there feels a sense of loss and which generates a lot of negativity. I hold in high esteem those leaders who demonstrate equality and fairness in all that they do."

Equality Hall of Fame...

- **Emmeline Pankhurst** — British suffragette and founder of the Women's Social and Political Union, who campaigned for women to be given the right to vote.

- **Eleanor Roosevelt** — Chair of the Presidential Commission on the Status of Women (1961–62), credited with helping launch the second wave of feminism.

- **William Wilberforce** — British politician, philanthropist, and leading activist for the abolition of slavery, heading the parliamentary campaign that led to the passage of the Slave Trade Act, 1807.

Equality in Relationships — What Works and What to Watch Out For...

You are known to be very fair to others. You are accepting of other people and tolerant of differences. You may get hung up on issues of fair treatment, so choose your battles wisely. People value you as a friend and colleague for your focus on equality and fairness, but you could leave people feeling uncomfortable if they stray outside of your own perspective on how things should be.

Equality at Work — Occupations Where You Could Find a Fit...

- Civil servant;
- International development worker;
- Judge;
- Mediator;
- Ombudsman.

Equality at Play — Leisure Suggestions You Might Enjoy...

- Advocacy;
- Board games;
- Blogging;
- Refereeing team sports;
- Volunteer police officer.

But Don't Take It Too Far...Equality Overplayed...

Don't just be equal for equality's sake! Your strength in paying great attention to issues of fairness and making sure that all people are treated equally can, if overplayed, hinder what is best for individuals or the situation. Focus, instead, on what is right for individuals — for their enjoyment, for their well-being, for their development — and what will deliver the best results for the situation.

Esteem Builder

People strong in Esteem Builder help others to believe in themselves and see what they are capable of achieving.

If You Have a Strength in Esteem Builder...

Your words and actions help to build self-confidence and self-esteem in others. You clearly see the potential and possibility in people and help them to recognise it for themselves. Through your relationships, you give people an understanding of what they are good at, even when they do not recognise it themselves. You love to help them to use this knowledge to build their confidence and self-esteem, and in turn to work towards achieving what they are capable of achieving.

The Esteem Builder Catchphrase...

"I knew you had it in you..."

Meet Jenny, strong in Esteem Builder...

"I hate people not believing in themselves and not fulfilling their potential. In my working life, a significant part of what I do is about supporting people to believe in themselves and to be what they can be. If I see a waste of human life, then it hurts. I am naturally people focused and my entire working life has been around people, helping them to believe in themselves more and to go on and achieve what they want."

Esteem Builder Hall of Fame...

- **Jane Addams** — Regarded as one of the founders of modern social work through her work in the U.S. Settlement House movement; first American woman to be awarded the Nobel Peace Prize for her international peace efforts.

- **Baloo the Bear** — Fictional bear in Rudyard Kipling's *The Jungle Book*; mentor of the boy Mowgli who continually helps Mowgli to believe that he can achieve what he wants to achieve.

- **Gok Wan** — British fashion consultant who has championed the cause of women feeling good about how they look naked.

Esteem Builder in Relationships — What Works and What to Watch Out For...

You are a generally positive person who does not hesitate to see the best in others. You are free with praise and compliments and it is important to you that others regard themselves well. Be aware that not everyone is immediately comfortable with public praise. You may need to learn how to tailor your praise-giving so that it is in the right way for people and at the right time.

Esteem Builder at Work — Occupations Where You Could Find a Fit...

- Careers advisor;
- Community worker;
- Nursery nurse;
- Prison officer;
- Social worker.

Esteem Builder at Play — Leisure Suggestions You Might Enjoy...

- Befriender;
- Childcare volunteer;
- Home theatre;
- Tutoring;
- Youth work volunteer.

But Don't Take It Too Far...Esteem Builder Overplayed...

Don't over-flatter! Your strength in seeing the possibility in other people and helping them to see what they are capable of can, if overplayed, be interpreted as obsequious and inauthentic. Be careful to maintain your authenticity as you help others to develop their self-belief.

Explainer

People strong in Explainer simplify things so that others can understand.

If You Have a Strength in Explainer...

You love to simplify things so that people can easily understand. You can take a complex idea and express it simply and clearly, making complicated ideas readily accessible to a wide range of people. If someone doesn't understand your explanation the first time, you will always try again, finding enjoyment from coming up with different ways of explaining the same thing.

The Explainer Catchphrase...

"How can I put it..."

Meet Yvonne, strong in Explainer...

"I work in an area that is really very technical and some of the things that we have to deal with on an everyday basis are actually quite mathematical. So you can imagine this tends to frighten a lot of people. What I love being able to do is to take some of the complicated technical stuff that we do, and present it in such a way that the people working for me understand it. I break things down, using simple language that everyone understands. I observe the people I am talking to a lot, seeing how they respond, keeping things as simple as they can be, and asking lots of questions just to make sure that they have got it."

Explainer Hall of Fame...

- **Malcolm Gladwell** — Staff writer with *The New Yorker magazine* and author of *The Tipping Point*; renowned for his ability to explain scientific and social concepts to a lay audience.

- **Susan Greenfield** — Director of the Royal Institution of Great Britain who was awarded the CBE for her contributions to the public understanding of science.

- **Delia Smith** — Best-selling UK cookery author who taught thousands of people to cook for themselves through her television series and cookery books.

Explainer in Relationships — What Works and What to Watch Out For...

You have a tendency to teach others. The world around you is full of fascination and you often want to share your interest with others through your explanations. Be aware that although people generally appreciate your ability to simplify complex information, not everyone shares all of your interests, or wants your explanations — especially all the time.

Explainer at Work — Occupations Where You Could Find a Fit...

- Driving instructor;
- Financial advisor;
- Spokesperson;
- Teacher;
- Technical support representative.

Explainer at Play — Leisure Suggestions You Might Enjoy...

- Astrology;
- Biography writing;
- Crosswords;
- Tutoring;
- Volunteer teacher.

But Don't Take It Too Far...Explainer Overplayed...

Don't patronise! Your strength in simplifying things and making complex ideas readily accessible so that people can understand them can, if overplayed, result in you explaining everything, to everyone, all the time. Learn to distinguish when — and to whom — things need explaining. Letting people work things out for themselves can be a valuable part of the learning process for them — don't deny them the opportunity!

Feedback

People strong in Feedback provide fair and accurate feedback to others to help them develop.

If You Have a Strength in Feedback...

You enjoy giving people both positive and negative feedback as appropriate. You believe that it is important for people to know what they have done well, so that they can build on it and progress. Equally, you let people know where they can improve, delivering this feedback accurately and constructively.

The Feedback Catchphrase...

"Can I have a word?"

Meet Daniel, strong in Feedback...

"Being open and honest with people is the only way to be, people appreciate you for it. I have to speak on a number of occasions to people about the way they are working, about how maybe they tend to ignore other parts of the business just to get their own way. Only the other day I had to speak to someone and be truthful and honest about what he was doing. It gave me the chance to impart some wisdom to him, I felt that not only was there a learning about dealing with people but also learning about the reality of the business world. He took my message to heart and sent a note out to his team. He wasn't looking at the bigger picture and providing leadership there. My feedback helped him to do that."

Feedback Hall of Fame...

- **Marva Collins** — American educator renowned for working with disadvantaged students, using the Socratic method of classical education, helping them to succeed and flourish.

- **Simon Cowell** — Television personality and judge on X Factor and American Idol; renowned for his direct feedback to contestants.

- **Alex Ferguson** — Manager of Manchester United Football Club, one of the most successful British football clubs in history; nicknamed "the hairdryer" for the feedback he gives his players.

Feedback in Relationships — What Works and What to Watch Out For...

You grow and change through the process of direct feedback and expect others to do the same. You have a habit of evaluating and commenting on other people's actions and decisions. To keep relationships healthy, solicit permission before you give people feedback — as they may not always welcome what you have to say!

Feedback at Work — Occupations Where You Could Find a Fit...

- Coach;
- Editor;
- Manager;
- Teacher;
- Trainer.

Feedback at Play — Leisure Suggestions You Might Enjoy...

- Blogging;
- Contest judge;
- Community magazine editor;
- Film critic;
- Team/individual coach.

But Don't Take It Too Far...Feedback Overplayed...

There's a time and a place! Your strength in providing fair and accurate feedback to others in order to help them develop can, if overplayed, lead you to provide feedback at inappropriate times or in inappropriate contexts. Know when to reign yourself back from giving feedback. Feedback is not *always* welcome — however much you think people might need it!

Gratitude

People strong in Gratitude are constantly thankful for the positive things in their lives.

If You Have a Strength in Gratitude...

You are constantly aware of how fortunate you are, and have a natural inclination to notice and feel appreciation for the good things that happen to you. You take nothing and no-one for granted. Each day, you feel privileged to be who you are and to do what you do, being grateful for the life you lead and the positive things within it.

The Gratitude Catchphrase...

"Thank you."

Meet Bob, strong in Gratitude...

"If something is going really well — it doesn't have to be something really big and spectacular — but maybe if everyone is happy working or playing well, I tend to have a little sigh of contentment to myself. What I suppose I do is to take timeout moments during the day, just to say thank you when things go well. I wish I could just capture those moments and bottle them up for the future. It doesn't take much to say thank you, and I find that I do it often throughout the course of the day."

Gratitude Hall of Fame...

- **Halle Berry** — Winner of the Best Actress Academy Award for her role in Monster's Ball (2001); renowned for her acceptance speech in which she expressed extensive gratitude to a long list of people who had supported her.

- **Robert Emmons** — American psychologist and leading gratitude researcher, including developing the GQ-6 gratitude questionnaire.

- **David Steindl-Rast** — Austrian-American theologian, recognised for his active participation in interfaith dialogue and renowned writer on the topic of gratitude.

Gratitude in Relationships — What Works and What to Watch Out For...

You often express your appreciation for others. You are good about thanking, praising, and complimenting. You tend not to take others for granted, and are uniquely suited to giving other people a little lift through your natural gratitude. Work on ensuring that your gratitude is always experienced by people as authentic, and that you don't slip into being seen as obsequious or insincere.

Gratitude at Work — Occupations Where You Could Find a Fit...

- County councillor;
- Fundraiser;
- Pathologist;
- Priest;
- Volunteer manager.

Gratitude at Play — Leisure Suggestions You Might Enjoy...

- Charity worker;
- Choir singing;
- Floral arranging;
- Hospice volunteer;
- Nature walks.

But Don't Take It Too Far...Gratitude Overplayed...

Don't give thanks without meaning your thanks authentically. Your strength in taking nothing for granted and for noticing and being thankful for the good things in life can, if overplayed, cause you to give thanks for everything. If this becomes blasé, it runs the risk of being perceived by others as insincere. Learn to moderate when, and how often, you show your appreciation, so that it always has the positive impact that you want it to have.

Growth

People strong in Growth are always looking for ways to grow and develop, whatever they are doing.

If You Have a Strength in Growth...

You actively seek out activities that will help you develop, whether they are new skills, new knowledge or a different way of doing things. You love to invite feedback on your performance, taking on board both positive and negative comments that will help you improve your performance and develop as a person.

The Growth Catchphrase...

"I learn something new every day."

Meet Cindy, strong in Growth...

"I feel as though I am successful when I am learning something new. I have always enjoyed taking photographs and every photograph I take I try to make it unique. Each shot that I take I learn something, it could be about the lighting, or the angles or even about the person I am taking the photograph of. I'm always looking to see if there are different ways that I can develop and improve my skills. More recently I volunteered to do some work experience at a local studio. Working there has taught me so much and I am in my element, I've learned how to organise a proper professional shoot, how to edit the photographs I take and even how to present them to the clients to gain business. The whole learning experience has been brilliant, I wouldn't swap it for anything."

Growth Hall of Fame...

- **Florence Bascom** — Only the second woman to be awarded a PhD in Geology, she went on to become the first woman to be part of the Geological Survey in 1896, and the first woman to hold any office (she was vice-president) in the Geological Survey of America.

- **Mihaly Csikszentmihalyi** — Hungarian-born polymath and author of numerous books, including *Flow: The Psychology of Optimal Experience.*
- **Socrates** — Greek philosopher who recognised that "The wise man is the man who knows how much he does not know."

Growth in Relationships — What Works and What to Watch Out For...

You are a growthful person and strive to improve yourself. In your relationships, you tend to set clear expectations and solicit feedback. You may feel frustrated with others who do not grow as readily as you do — but learn how to give them space and time, while simultaneously trying to balance your own needs for growth and development.

Growth at Work — Occupations Where You Could Find a Fit...

- Entrepreneur;
- Musician;
- Research scientist;
- Scholar;
- Sportsperson.

Growth at Play — Leisure Suggestions You Might Enjoy...

- Documentary watching;
- Educational visits;
- Reading;
- Sports;
- Study and learning.

But Don't Take It Too Far...Growth Overplayed...

Don't be selfish! Your strength in focusing actively on your personal growth and development can, if overplayed, result in you becoming self-absorbed as you pursue one growthful experience after another. Find a balance that takes into account others' needs and interests, particularly those closest to you, or your colleagues with whom you work most closely.

Humility

People strong in Humility are happy to stay in the background, preferring others to be recognised and to take credit for their contributions.

If You Have a Strength in Humility...

You are a humble person, never allowing yourself to be big-headed or boastful. Although you feel satisfaction with a job well done, you tend to give other people credit for your successes rather than take the credit yourself. You know how much you depend on others for your accomplishments, and you appreciate and value their help and support.

The Humility Catchphrase...

"No, no, I don't deserve the credit, it was all down to..."

Meet Sally, strong in Humility...

"The school where I teach drama has just put on an amazing show. The kids have worked incredibly hard and I feel very honoured to be part of the production team, we have some really bright and talented children. I know that the success is down to their hard work and commitment, and that my role has only been a small part. So when people come up and congratulate me, I feel a bit uncomfortable and I am quick to point out that it is because of the kids' hard work that the show was such a success. I know deep within myself that what I contribute is valuable, but I don't think that I am better than anyone else and I certainly would never describe myself as being very good at anything."

Humility Hall of Fame...

- **Susan Boyle** — Scottish singer who came to public attention when she appeared on *Britain's Got Talent*, her exceptional singing voice contrasting with her plain appearance on stage.

- **David Robinson** — Co-Founder of Community Links and Vice-Chair of the Council on Social Action — yet you will struggle to find his profile on the Community Links website.

- **Darwin Smith** — Former Chairman and Chief Executive of Kimberley-Clark, credited with building the company into a consumer products giant.

Humility in Relationships — What Works and What to Watch Out For...

You are easy for others to get along with because your ego rarely interferes with your relationships. You are fair about sharing credit as well as blame. Be careful not to let others take advantage of you or overlook your contribution just because you don't blow your own trumpet.

Humility at Work — Occupations Where You Could Find a Fit...

- Art therapist;
- Florist;
- Hospice worker;
- Nurse;
- Priest.

Humility at Play — Leisure Suggestions You Might Enjoy...

- Calligraphy;
- Coin collecting;
- Gardening;
- Model building;
- Volunteering.

But Don't Take It Too Far...Humility Overplayed...

Don't hide your light! Your strength in appreciating, valuing, and giving credit to other people for successes rather than taking the credit yourself can, if overplayed, mean that you never take credit for your own contributions. This could result in others never appreciating your contribution, nor appreciating your potential and what you could bring. Learn to balance your humility with being confident to talk about your achievements, even just occasionally — you risk missing opportunities otherwise.

Humour

People strong in Humour see the funny side of almost everything that happens — and make a joke of it.

If You Have a Strength in Humour...

You love making people laugh and look for every opportunity to do it. You are able see the funny side of things and like to share this funny side with others. You have the ability to crack a joke or tell a story that lightens the mood, gives enjoyment to others and helps people relax.

The Humour Catchphrase...

"Have you heard the one about..."

Meet Michaela, strong in Humour...

"I have one particular fear, spiders! I am actually terrified of them and avoid at all costs going anywhere that I might come into contact with one. But I always make light of it and somehow turn my fears into one huge joke. You can imagine that a school field trip, going pond dipping, was not on my list of things to do. But I had to go and it turned out that we had a great time. I made everyone laugh with my stupid antics at avoiding doing anything that involved putting my hands into dark, slimy water, and checking under my bed every night for creepy crawlies. I must admit that I can make any situation seem funny — I just love making people laugh."

Humour Hall of Fame...

- **Ronnie Barker and Ronnie Corbett** — Together, *The Two Ronnies*, icons of British comedy.

- **Tina Fey** — Satirist, screenwriter, and television star; creator of award-winning *30 Rock* and former head writer for *Saturday Night Live*.

- **Dawn French and Jennifer Saunders** – British comediennes, most famous for writing and starring in the comedy sketch show, *French and Saunders*.

Humour in Relationships – What Works and What to Watch Out For...

There's no getting around it: you are funny. You often put people at ease with your humour and have a knack for dispelling tense situations. You may like to be the centre of attention. Remember to use this gift wisely as overdoing humour can interfere with the sanctity or seriousness of certain moments or situations.

Humour at Work – Occupations Where You Could Find a Fit...

- Bartender;
- Children's television presenter;
- Comedian/comedienne;
- Party planner;
- Trainer.

Humour at Play – Leisure Suggestions You Might Enjoy...

- Hula hooping;
- Juggling;
- Party hosting;
- Stand-up comedy;
- Theatre.

But Don't Take It Too Far...Humour Overplayed...

Know when humour is not funny! Your strength in using humour to make people laugh, to help people relax, and to lighten the mood can, if overplayed, cause others never to take you seriously. Learn to spot when humour is not welcome, or might have a negative impact. Develop strategies for reining back your desire always to deliver the punchline at these times.

Improver

People strong in Improver constantly look for better ways of doing things, for how things can be improved.

If You Have a Strength in Improver...

You do not tend to accept the way things are usually done, but instead get a thrill from seeing how you can make things more effective. You love looking for ways to do things better. You have an innate sense of how to improve on any way of doing things, and find that you do this quite naturally — all of the time.

The Improver Catchphrase...

"This can be done better if we do it this way..."

Meet Sandra, strong in Improver...

"I have a bit of reputation of being good with processes, standardising processes and part of that involves taking something that isn't working as well as it could and making it either simpler, or clearer, or more logical, or more efficient. But I don't have to be told when to improve something — it seems to be something that I just naturally do. One job I had involved people working a shift pattern, to give 24 hour cover, 7 days a week for 365 days per year. I had heard that there was some tension around the structure of the shift pattern and so within a year, even though I was still only a junior employee, I had put in a proposal to restructure the way that the staff worked. I think it is a bit unusual to do that and I wasn't sure how it would be received — but within a month it had been taken on and it was seen as the way forward."

Improver Hall of Fame...

- **Mary Anderson** — inventor of the windscreen wiper, for which she was awarded a US patent in 1903, thereby improving the driving experience and safety of millions.

- **Elizabeth Fry** — English humanitarian known for her activism for prison reform; since 2002 she has been depicted on the Bank of England £5 note.
- **Jack Welch** — Renowned CEO of GE plc, always striving for greater efficiency and higher profits.

Improver in Relationships — What Works and What to Watch Out For...

You are likely to have relationships that are "in flux". You are always on the lookout for new ways to connect with others and experience your friendships. Be sure to keep those strategies that work, however, and be careful not to let good friends go just because you think you can do even better.

Improver at Work — Occupations Where You Could Find a Fit...

- Architect;
- Engineer;
- Inventor;
- Restaurateur;
- Software designer.

Improver at Play — Leisure Suggestions You Might Enjoy...

- Car maintenance;
- Civic/community volunteer;
- Do-it-yourself home improvements;
- Inventing;
- Model building.

But Don't Take It Too Far...Improver Overplayed...

Know when to leave well alone! Your strength in seeing how things can be done better and in suggesting and making improvements can, if overplayed, mean you never rest or accept that things are sufficient or satisfactory. For some, this will be deeply frustrating. Learn to spot when something does not need refining or improving, but can safely be left as-is — and then relax!

Incubator

People strong in Incubator love to think deeply about things over time, pondering and reflecting to arrive at the best conclusion.

If You Have a Strength in Incubator...

You love to think, to ponder, to reflect. This ability to think things through is a constant throughout your day — every day. You like to take moments out of your day, your week, or your month to give yourself dedicated thinking time; to think deeply about things. These times are very precious to you, allowing you the time and space to be absorbed in your own thoughts without annoying distractions.

The Incubator Catchphrase...

"I'll mull that over..."

Meet Isaiah, strong in Incubator...

"I love having conversations with people and then being able to think about it and reflect. It takes a little while so I might chew it over, contemplate it, ponder it, think about it, reflect on it. I often do that subconsciously, so I often enjoy giving myself time to hold something a while and not consciously work on it at all — and then come back to it later. I have just done this with a new approach to training courses. I spent some time thinking about how my approach might work in practice, bounced ideas around in my own mind and with other people, and then I put the proposal together — and it worked really well."

Incubator Hall of Fame...

- **Dorothy Hodgkin** — Winner of the Nobel Prize for Chemistry, she deciphered the structure of insulin after 35 years of work.

- **Isambard Kingdom Brunel** — British engineer best known for his creation of the Great Western Railway; he reputedly would retire to bed and sleep on difficult engineering problems.

- **Jose Saramago** – Recipient of the Nobel Prize in Literature; he did not write his first novel until he was in his mid-50s.

Incubator in Relationships – What Works and What to Watch Out For...

Your strength in Incubator may be easily confused with procrastination; as a result, other people might get frustrated with you. Be sure to explain your work style and rest assured: in the long run, your friends, family members and colleagues will learn to trust you as you take your time to think things through.

Incubator at Work – Occupations Where You Could Find a Fit...

- Artist;
- Feature journalist;
- Inventor;
- Museum curator;
- Scientist.

Incubator at Play – Leisure Suggestions You Might Enjoy...

- Cloud watching;
- Fishing;
- Kite flying;
- Sudoku;
- Swimming.

But Don't Take It Too Far...Incubator Overplayed...

Don't ponder everything! Your strength in taking time to reflect and to think things through to come to the best conclusion can, if overplayed, mean you come across as self-absorbed and unresponsive. Not everyone will need or want time to reflect – some people prefer to move quickly to action. Learn to spot when a more nimble, less reflective approach is necessary.

Innovation

People strong in Innovation continually approach things in original and ingenious ways, striving to come up with new and different approaches and applications.

If You Have a Strength in Innovation...

You are driven by the desire to want to design and create things that are better than what has been done before. You have the ability to look at things from a different perspective to others, to think laterally and "out of the box". You don't get blinkered by what exists now, but rather you look beyond this and into the realms of what could be. Your ideas and inventions help move things forward, improving on what previously existed through your insight and application.

The Innovation Catchphrase...

"A tweak here, a twist there..."

Meet Joseph, strong in Innovation...

"I've always been a trier and a tweaker, as far back as I can remember. As a child, I remember taking things to pieces and then putting them back together to see if I could get them to work better. I still do it now — whether it's physical things, like the toaster, or whether it's ideas from work about how to improve that product, or how we can provide a better service. I am always trying out things from scratch, coming up with ideas that have never been tried before, and seeing what I can do to get them to work. Sometimes it takes years for an idea to come to fruition — but it doesn't matter, they're always there, bubbling along in the background. Other times, the ideas come quicker and I know just what I need to do to make something work."

Innovation Hall of Fame...

- **Jacqueline Gold** — Chief Executive of Ann Summers, and originator of the concept of women-only home party plans as a means to sell and distribute Ann Summers products.

- **Mary Kies** — First woman to be granted a US patent, in 1809, for a technique of weaving straw with silk and thread, used in hat-making.

- **Leonardo da Vinci** — Italian artist, anatomist, and inventor; widely credited as being the one of the most innovative people in the history of the world.

Innovation in Relationships — What Works and What to Watch Out For...

You are always on the lookout for new ways to interact with people. You enjoy trying out new activities and ways to connect. In your race for innovation don't forget that you can also rely on the tried and tested from time to time....especially where long-term relationships are concerned!

Innovation at Work — Occupations Where You Could Find a Fit...

- Advertising executive;
- Engineer;
- Inventor;
- Product developer;
- Web designer.

Innovation at Play — Leisure Suggestions You Might Enjoy...

- Cooking;
- Inventing;
- Painting;
- Tinkering;
- Wine making.

But Don't Take It Too Far...Innovation Overplayed...

Don't innovate for the sake of it! Your strength in being able to look at things from a different perceptive and come up with new ways of doing things can, if overplayed, be obstructive rather than constructive. There's a time and a place for lateral thinking. Learn to spot when your desire for innovation is going to be a hindrance rather than a help.

Judgement

People strong in Judgement enjoy making decisions and are able to make the right decision quickly and easily.

If You Have a Strength in Judgement...

You make decisions quickly and easily. You enjoy quickly assessing the evidence of any situation and are confident that you will reach the right decision through your rapid analysis and weighing of the facts. You take pride in the fact that your decisions stand up to robust challenge, and usually turn out to be right.

The Judgement Catchphrase...

"On balance, it seems to me that..."

Meet Gary, strong in Judgement...

"I manage to keep all the salient points uppermost in my mind. Students come to me everyday asking me for my advice about anything from which accommodation is best to which experiments they should be doing. One of my students, who works particularly hard, was debating about doing one of two experiments. Both could have thrown up some interesting results, but I advised that the first one would be better in terms of time and results. He got some pretty amazing readings which we hope to share with everyone at the next conference."

Judgement Hall of Fame...

- **Confucius** — Chinese philosopher whose teachings can be found in the *Analects of Confucius*.

- **King Solomon** — Described in the Bible as the King of Israel, revered for his wisdom and the legend of the Judgement of Solomon, in which he adjudicated who was the true mother of a disputed baby.

- **Sandra Day O'Connor** — first female member of the United States Supreme Court.

Judgement in Relationships — What Works and What to Watch Out For...

You are a critical thinker and this means that you are at ease with the idea of evaluating others. You have clear standards and know immediately when other people fail to meet them. Remember, however, that everyone makes mistakes and that you might work better with others if you extend them a second chance when they need it.

Judgement at Work — Occupations Where You Could Find a Fit...

- Actuary;
- Investment analyst;
- Medical practitioner;
- Judge;
- Recruitment consultant.

Judgement at Play — Leisure Suggestions You Might Enjoy...

- Antiques collecting;
- Chess;
- Poker;
- Stamp collecting;
- Stock market investment.

But Don't Take It Too Far...Judgement Overplayed...

Don't be closed to wider perspectives! Your strength in deploying sound judgement and making the right decisions can, if overplayed, leave you closed to wider opinions or perspectives. Make time to seek and incorporate the views and opinions of others and use this to refine your own decision-making processes.

Legacy

People strong in Legacy want to create things that will outlast them, delivering a sustainable positive impact after they have gone.

If You Have a Strength in Legacy...

You care deeply about future generations and seek to leave a legacy through what you do. You enjoy working on things that make a difference and will have a positive impact on others. In whatever you do, you want to ensure that you create something that will outlast you and continues to make a positive contribution after you have gone.

The Legacy Catchphrase...

"My work will live on..."

Meet Bill, strong in Legacy...

"What I leave behind is so important to me. I was told when I was young that you should always aim to leave the world a better place when you leave it to when you entered it — and that has stayed with me all through my life. In everything I do, I'm thinking about the impact it will have on the people who follow me. It's so easy to look at the negative impacts that our generation is leaving for the next — environmental damage, global warming, terrorism and security issues — but I want to make sure I leave something positive that I can pass on, and that, in turn can be passed on by them. I've learned so much from people who are now passed away, but who left their ideas behind in books and things they wrote. That's the single biggest reason that I write, and the single biggest reason that I teach — because I want to pass my legacy on to the next generations."

Legacy Hall of Fame...

- **Vint Cerf** — American computer scientist and the person most often called "The Father of the Internet;" credited with developing the TCP/IP technology that enables internet communication.

- **Wangari Muta Maathai** — Founder of the Kenyan Green Belt Movement, an environmental organisation focused on planting trees, environmental conservation, and women's rights.

- **Michael Young** — Founder of the Open University, which has gone on to educate millions of people who may not otherwise have had access to education.

Legacy in Relationships — What Works and What to Watch Out For...

You are especially likely to connect with those "under" you, whether they are people you supervise at work or younger family members. Your focus is on your impact in your relationships, and how you can ensure that your impact continues to be positive long after you have gone.

Legacy at Work — Occupations Where You Could Find a Fit...

- Charity worker;
- Environmental activist;
- Philanthropist;
- Stay-at-home parent;
- Teacher.

Legacy at Play — Leisure Suggestions You Might Enjoy...

- Antiques collecting;
- Gardening;
- Genealogy;
- Home renovation;
- Youth work volunteer.

But Don't Take It Too Far...Legacy Overplayed...

Don't become a slave to the future! Your strength in caring deeply about future generations and focusing your effort on things that will leave a lasting legacy can, if overplayed, limit the extent to which you live in the present. Balance your focus on your cause or the creation of your legacy, with an ability to relax and "enjoy the moment" from time to time — you deserve it!

Listener

People strong in Listener are able to focus on and listen intently to what people say.

If You Have a Strength in Listener...

You show a keen interest in what people have to say and the way that they say it. When people are speaking to you, you focus intently — on them and on what they are saying. You listen not only to the words, but to how those words are used. Everything that someone says is important — you don't miss a thing.

The Listener Catchphrase...

"Uh-hmm..."

Meet Janet, strong in Listener...

"Listening to someone closely is one of the biggest compliments that you can pay to anyone. Everyone just loves to be listened to, and I just love to do that for people. I find everyone interesting. I used to live on a street with lots of terraced houses, some of which were converted into flats and occupied by a wide variety of people — young professionals, families, and lots of elderly people. I just loved listening to all their stories, I found everyone fascinating. A trip to the local shops at the bottom of the road was a pure delight to me. Each trip could last a number of hours because I would always find someone to talk to — or rather to listen to! When I am listening, I focus completely and utterly on the person talking — they know that I am listening. It seems like I shut out the entire world except for them and what they are saying. Time just flies by."

Listener Hall of Fame...

- **Stephen Covey** — Advocate of listening through "Seek first to understand, then to be understood" in *The Seven Habits of Highly Effective People*.
- **Samaritans** — Charity founded in 1953 to provide telephone-based emotional support to people who are in distress or at risk of suicide.

- **Xian Zhang** — Orchestra conductor appointed the first female music director of the Giuseppe Verdi Orchestra in Milan, Italy; the first woman to hold such a position in an Italian symphony orchestra.

Listener in Relationships — What Works and What to Watch Out For...

You are highly receptive to others. You have little trouble paying attention and are dependable in your ability to support or appreciate others. You prefer to be the listener rather than to be the centre of attention, and this makes you a good friend to have around. Remember, though, that like communication, relationships are two-way, so you need to talk sometimes as well as listening.

Listener at Work — Occupations Where You Could Find a Fit...

- Customer service advisor;
- Mental health support worker;
- Sound engineer;
- Speech and language therapist;
- Talk show host.

Listener at Play — Leisure Suggestions You Might Enjoy...

- Child reading volunteer;
- Crisis volunteer;
- Disc jockeying;
- Listening to music;
- Symphony orchestra.

But Don't Take It Too Far...Listener Overplayed...

Know when not to shut up! Your strength in listening intently to others and showing a keen interest in what they have to say can, if overplayed, stifle interpersonal communication. Communication is a two-way process — know when to shift from listener to speaker, in order to help maintain a smooth dialogue with people and be an active part of what is going on.

Mission

People strong in Mission pursue things which give them a sense of meaning and purpose, always working toward a longer-term goal.

If You Have a Strength in Mission...

You derive great fulfilment from pursuing activities which give your life meaning and purpose. The focus of your purpose could be one — or more than one — of many different things — but whatever it is, you are committed to pursuing it, totally and completely. How you spend your time, the decisions you make, the plans you have for the future — all are aligned to your overriding sense of mission and purpose in life.

The Mission Catchphrase...

"Do what matters — because nothing else does."

Meet Desmond, strong in Mission...

"I just love to follow my heart and do things which are really worthwhile and which give a real sense of meaning to people's lives. I am committed to working for the benefit of others, to making their lives more enjoyable and for this enjoyment to be sustainable. This is at the heart of everything I do, and I have to be this way. In this respect, the job I am involved with at the moment absolutely allows me to do this without any restraints. For this reason I just feel so lucky to be working for them and would actually work for them for no pay because it means that much to me."

Mission Hall of Fame...

- **Camila Batmanghelidjh** — Founder of the children's charity Kids Company, which works to provide disadvantaged children with better life chances.

- **Anita Roddick** — British businesswoman, environmentalist, and founder of *The Body Shop*, a producer and retailer of cosmetic products that shaped ethical consumerism.

- **Muhammad Yunus** — Founder of Grameen Bank and Nobel Peace Prize Winner.

Mission in Relationships — What Works and What to Watch Out For...

Your sense of mission and commitment to a cause can be fantastic if it is shared by the people in your relationships. If it isn't, though, be mindful that they could be left feeling isolated and out of touch, since your energy and attention will almost always be drawn to the mission you are pursuing. One way of guarding against this could be to make your relationships a focus of your strength in mission...

Mission at Work — Occupations Where You Could Find a Fit...

- Activist;
- Charity worker;
- Priest;
- Scientist;
- Youth worker.

Mission at Play — Leisure Suggestions You Might Enjoy...

- Child advocacy;
- Community activist;
- Environmental activism;
- Volunteering;
- Youth development.

But Don't Take It Too Far...Mission Overplayed...

Don't let your mission be the only mission! Your strength in aligning your plans, your decisions, and your time according to your overriding sense of mission and life purpose can, if overplayed, dominate everything you do. Not everyone will share or support your mission. Know when to contribute to helping others achieve their own mission or life goals. Try to be flexible in not focusing on your own mission to the exclusion of everyone and everything else. Instead, flex your style — and enjoy giving yourself a "mission break" from time to time!

Moral Compass

People strong in Moral Compass are guided by their strong ethical code, always acting and making decisions in accordance with what they believe is right.

If You Have a Strength in Moral Compass...

You are a very moral person with an extremely strong ethical code. You are very aware of the difference between right and wrong and always act in accordance with what you believe is right. You are clear on your values and your moral reasoning for what you do and why you do it. Your decisions and your actions are always guided by your ethics and values, and you never step outside of these.

The Moral Compass Catchphrase...

"I just have to do the right thing..."

Meet Keith, strong in Moral Compass...

"At football at university one week their winger was just running rings around me, and my captain came over and told me to kick him. I said that you can drop me before I would do that. I don't care what you say, I'm not doing it, full stop. I don't mind being kicked, but I am just not going to kick anybody. I always stand by that sort of thing, because things come back to haunt you in the end. It just felt right. You get to a point where your own personal position becomes almost irrelevant. If there are consequences of what you do by doing the right thing, then so be it."

Moral Compass Hall of Fame...

- **Martin Bell** — Former BBC war reporter who argued that the neutral reporting of armed conflicts did a disservice to viewers when it was clear that atrocities were being committed; later stood as an independent MP to protest against "sleaze" in politics.

- **Rosa Parks** — African-American civil rights activist who sparked the Montgomery Bus Boycott by refusing to give up her seat for a white passenger, which she did as a private citizen who was "tired of giving in".

- **Jeffrey Wigand** — Former Vice President of Research and Development at tobacco company Brown & Williamson; renowned as a whistleblower who betrayed harmful industry practices to the public when he appeared on the CBS news programme, *60 Minutes*.

Moral Compass in Relationships — What Works and What to Watch Out For...

You will have a very clear view of what you will accept and what you will not tolerate from others. This can make you a steadfast friend, but also leaves you prone to intransigence, so be mindful of when it might be appropriate to flex your attitude and when not. Relationships are often built on a degree of give-and-take.

Moral Compass at Work — Occupations Where You Could Find a Fit...

- Campaigner;
- Chief Financial Officer;
- Headteacher;
- Journalistic film maker;
- Security guard.

Moral Compass at Play — Leisure Suggestions You Might Enjoy...

- Contest judge;
- Meditation;
- Referee/umpire;
- Police volunteer;
- Youth offender volunteer.

But Don't Take It Too Far...Moral Compass Overplayed...

Don't be righteous! Your strength in being clear on your values and moral code, and acting in keeping with them can, if overplayed, lead you to judge others strictly by your own standards. Not everyone will live their life by the same values and moral code as you do. Be open to learning from others about what is important to them.

Narrator

People strong in Narrator love to tell stories.

If You Have a Strength in Narrator...

You have a tremendous love of story. Telling stories comes very naturally to you. Even as ordinary events happen, you can picture how they might be spun into an anecdote or story for you tell others. You love to answer questions in the form of a story, and see the power of stories to convey morals, insights, values, humour, and many other lessons. For you, life is one big story waiting to be told.

The Narrator Catchphrase...

"Let me tell you a story about that..."

Meet David, strong in Narrator...

"I'm constantly amazed at the way people manage to conquer all sorts of adversities to do something extraordinary. I was trying to get this across to a group of people in a recent meeting, so to illustrate my point I showed them one of my most treasured possessions — a very beautiful model of a motorbike, received as a gift from a friend in South Africa. I told them the story of how the bike was created by people who probably had nothing of material wealth, from bits of old scrap wire and bin liners, and how they manage to create many beautiful things from things that people in the developed, wealthy countries would probably discard as rubbish."

Narrator Hall of Fame...

- **Aesop** — A slave and story-teller who lived in ancient Greece, credited with some of the most well-known fables in the world.

- **Dick Hill** — Renowned narrator of over 200 titles, who has earned three "Audie Awards" and was named a "Golden Voice" by AudioFile Magazine.

- **J.K. Rowling** — Author of the international best-selling *Harry Potter* fantasy series, which has sold more than 400 million copies worldwide.

Narrator in Relationships — What Works and What to Watch Out For...

You are a natural storyteller. You relate to others by talking about your own experiences or by learning about theirs. For you, relationships are an opportunity to trade stories. Your deepest emotional connections come from hearing the personal narratives of others and sharing your own.

Narrator at Work — Occupations Where You Could Find a Fit...

- Advertising executive;
- Author;
- Children's television presenter;
- Film/theatre director;
- Playgroup assistant.

Narrator at Play — Leisure Suggestions You Might Enjoy...

- Blogging;
- Hosting dinner parties;
- Storytelling to children;
- Theatre performances;
- Writing for local community newspapers.

But Don't Take It Too Far...Narrator Overplayed...

Don't become a story bore! Your strength in using stories and anecdotes to relate everyday events and answer questions can, if overplayed, be wearing for others. Know when a short or succinct response will be more appropriate than a lengthy narrative or story.

Optimism

People strong in Optimism always maintain a positive attitude and outlook on life.

If You Have a Strength in Optimism...

You always see the best side of any situation, with a consistent and firm belief that things will work out well in the future. Having this constant belief keeps you strong and enables you to stay positive even when things become difficult. You always look on the bright side of life.

The Optimism Catchphrase...

"Always look on the bright side of life..."

Meet Cara, strong in Optimism...

"Over the last couple of months I haven't really known what job I am going into next. You think that might have made me a bit insecure, but for some strange reason it hasn't. People around me have been moping about, complaining about this, that, and the other, but not me. I know that I am good at what I do, that something will turn up. I think you have to think positive and that is what I do, always."

Optimism Hall of Fame...

- **Anne Frank** — Dutch Jew who hid with her family in a secret attic until they were discovered and sent to concentration camps; famous for her diary, *The Diary of Anne Frank*.

- **Dr. Pangloss** — Eternally optimistic character in Voltaire's novel *Candide*.

- **Barbara Windsor** — British actress famous for starring in the Carry On films and as Peggy Mitchell in BBC's Eastenders; renowned for her upbeat personality and sunny disposition.

Optimism in Relationships — What Works and What to Watch Out For...

You generally have a positive disposition and this makes you very likeable. You tend to get along well with others and your natural optimism can be contagious. Remember, however, to allow those around you to feel sadness and disappointment where appropriate — and be careful not to allow people to take advantage of you in relationships, given your optimistic nature.

Optimism at Work — Occupations Where You Could Find a Fit...

• Crisis centre worker;
• Political activist;
• Rehabilitation worker;
• Salesperson;
• Trader.

Optimism at Play — Leisure Suggestions You Might Enjoy...

• Beachcombing;
• Butterfly watching;
• Competition entering;
• Hiking;
• Sailing.

But Don't Take It Too Far...Optimism Overplayed...

Don't be unrealistic! Your strength in maintaining an optimistic outlook and expecting things to work out well can, if overplayed, lead you to have unrealistic expectations or miss problems that should have been averted. While your natural optimism will help you persevere, remember that there are times when it is necessary to give up and that failure can also be an important experience.

Order

People strong in Order are exceptionally well-organised in everything they do.

If You Have a Strength in Order...

You love to be exceptionally well-organised. Everything has its place, both in your work and your personal life. Your order and organisation mean that you are able to be as effective as possible in everything you do. You always know where things are, what to do when, and why something is important — because you have answered these questions and organised everything in advance.

The Order Catchphrase...

"Everything has its place."

Meet Robin, strong in Order...

"If I think about work typically, and also aspects of outside life, I am very organised. I like things to be organised, bank records and so on, I like to have them filed clearly. My CD collection is well organised so I know where my music is. I have a big pile of CDs on my desk now, some of which I haven't even opened which is terrible. In fact, I'm going to have to go and sort them out now..."

Order Hall of Fame...

- **Betty Boothroyd** — First and (to date) only female Speaker of the British House of Commons, from 1992–2000; renowned for calling "Order, order!" to bring the House to order.

- **Abraham Ortelius** — Flemish cartographer who is generally recognised as the creator of the first modern atlas.

- **Kim Woodburn & Aggie MacKenzie** — stars of the hit British television show *How Clean is Your House?*, in which they visit dirty homes and clean them.

Order in Relationships — What Works and What to Watch Out For...

You tend to be predictable and this makes it easy for people to depend upon and relate to you. Remember, however, that other people may crave spontaneity. You may occasionally be stretched in your relationships by people who want more flexibility through the thrill of not knowing what is coming next. Allow yourself to be open to possibilities, and to be patient with people who are not as organised as you are!

Order at Work — Occupations Where You Could Find a Fit...

- Cleaner;
- Librarian;
- Personal assistant (PA);
- Pharmacist;
- Railway signal operator.

Order at Play — Leisure Suggestions You Might Enjoy...

- Calligraphy;
- Community clean-up volunteer;
- Embroidery;
- Genealogy;
- Sudoku.

But Don't Take It Too Far...Order Overplayed...

Know when to allow disorder! Your strength in being extremely well-organised and having a place for everything can, if overplayed, come across as overly constraining to others. It may also limit the extent to which you are able to be open to other possibilities. Not everyone enjoys structure and order. Be prepared to relax your focus to engage others — and be open to new information or ideas to ensure that you can focus your efforts at bringing order appropriately.

Persistence

People strong in Persistence achieve success by keeping going even when things are difficult.

If You Have a Strength in Persistence...

You pride yourself on being able to keep going in the face of difficult challenges, frustrations and seemingly insurmountable problems. You understand that success in the face of adversity requires extra effort and determination, so you never give up.

The Persistence Catchphrase...

"Never, ever, ever give up."

Meet Alison, strong in Persistence...

"I work mainly with young people and one day last year, the mother of one of my young people died and I desperately wanted to travel to Manchester to see him. Unfortunately, on the day I was due to travel, it snowed heavily overnight. Most of where I live ground to a halt, the narrow country lane where I live was virtually impassable. But I was determined to make the journey. To get out of the driveway, I had to shovel the snow away from the wheels of the car, foot by foot, so that I could go forwards. Then, on the lane, I had to shovel snow every few metres to overcome the pot holes and slopes. Some people did stop to help, but most left after 15 minutes saying that it was impossible and to just "Call it a day". But I was determined and just kept going. It took me about 3 hours, but I did it, I got out of the drive and the country lane and onto the motorway."

Persistence Hall of Fame...

- **Ellen MacArthur** — British sailor and world record holder for fastest solo circumnavigation of the world in a seacraft.
- **Major Phil Packer** — British army veteran who sustained serious spinal cord injuries while serving in Iraq; went on to row across the English Channel, complete the London Marathon in 14 days, and haul himself 3,000ft up El Capitan mountain in California, raising £1.2 million for charity; winner of The Pride of Britain Award 2009 for Fundraiser of the Year.

- **Cha Sa-Soon** — 68 year old Korean woman who has failed her driving theory test no less than 950 times — but still has continued to turn up almost every weekday to re-take the test. Unfortunately for her, when she passes the theory test she will then be faced with the practical driving test — good luck!

Persistence in Relationships — What Works and What to Watch Out For...

You are a loyal friend. You don't give up on people just because there has been an argument or because you do not immediately understand their needs or wants. Be careful, however, as your persistence can also prolong arguments if you allow it to become stubbornness. Watch for how you can use your persistence as a virtue in relationships, rather than letting it slide into being a vice!

Persistence at Work — Occupations Where You Could Find a Fit...

- Actor/actress;
- Advocate;
- Detective;
- Fundraiser;
- Humanitarian aid worker.

Persistence at Play — Leisure Suggestions You Might Enjoy...

- Bird watching;
- Deep sea fishing;
- Golf;
- Learning a musical instrument;
- Marathon running.

But Don't Take It Too Far...Persistence Overplayed...

Don't bark up the wrong tree! Your strength in achieving success by pushing yourself on, can, if overplayed, be misguided. Balance your persistence with an ability to judge when to give up and focus your efforts elsewhere. Sometimes withdrawal is the better option than persistence.

Personal Responsibility

People strong in Personal Responsibility take ownership of their decisions and hold themselves accountable for what they have promised to do.

If You Have a Strength in Personal Responsibility...

You are always true to your word. If you make a promise or commitment, then you make sure that you keep it. You never blame others, but take ownership of everything that you do and hold yourself accountable for doing it. You are seen as someone who takes responsibility for themselves, always being prepared to do what you have promised and what needs to be done.

The Personal Responsibility Catchphrase...

"You can count on me."

Meet Jasmine, strong in Personal Responsibility...

"I like being held answerable for anything that I do. From the smallest thing, like doing the post, to the bigger projects that I am sometimes asked to do. Like the other day I was asked to chase up some enquiries and I enjoyed doing that, I made sure that I had done them by the end of the day. I also make sure that when I promise to ring someone back within a certain timescale I always do, even if it means staying late. I would always make sure it is done, so that I can go away and think that is sorted, and the notes are clear so that anyone else following on from me knows what has happened."

Personal Responsibility Hall of Fame...

- **Viktor Frankl** — "The Statue of Liberty on the East Coast [should] be supplemented by a Statue of Responsibility on the West Coast."

- **Lawrence Oates** — Walked out to his deliberate death so as not to hold up Scott of the Antarctic on their expedition to the South Pole.

- **Irena Sendler** — Polish Catholic social worker who served in the Polish Underground during the Second World War, and saved more than 2,500 Jewish children by smuggling them out of the Warsaw ghetto.

Personal Responsibility in Relationships — What Works and What to Watch Out For...

You have a tendency to be forthcoming and honest. You earn the respect of others because of your ability to own up to mistakes and make changes. On the other hand, you expect others to have the same high level of personal accountability — and they may not. You may have to be patient with some people who are not immediately up to your high standards, but nonetheless, people will experience you as a solid and reliable friend and colleague.

Personal Responsibility at Work — Occupations Where You Could Find a Fit...

- Banker;
- Customer complaints advisor;
- Driver/courier;
- Lighthouse keeper;
- Residential warden.

Personal Responsibility at Play — Leisure Suggestions You Might Enjoy...

- Gardening;
- Parachuting;
- Pets;
- Team sports;
- Volunteering.

But Don't Take It Too Far...Personal Responsibility Overplayed...

Don't beat yourself up! Your strength in taking personal responsibility for things and always following through on your commitments can, if overplayed, impact negatively on your health, well-being and relationships. Allow others to take responsibility, and learn to balance your promises with the other important things in life.

Personalisation

People strong in Personalisation recognise everyone as an individual, noticing the subtle differences that make them unique.

If You Have a Strength in Personalisation...

You notice the subtle differences in people that make everyone unique. You recognise the different motivators of different people, as well as their likes, dislikes, preferences, strengths and talents. You appreciate that to get the best out of a person, you need to treat them as an individual. You love to relate to everyone as a unique individual, recognising that what is right for one person may well be wrong for another, and focusing your attention accordingly.

The Personalisation Catchphrase...

"Each to his or her own..."

Meet Sarah, strong in Personalisation...

"I have some staff that are very creative but I also have others that maybe are not so much creative but are pretty good 'doers'. In fact, even amongst the creative ones and the 'doers,' everybody is different and unique in their own way. One of my strengths is being able to ascertain what a person's unique capabilities are and what they are good at. I do this by observing them, you observe them for a period of time, give them certain challenges and get them to respond. I have some 'doers' who are very much self-starters and who I can pretty much guarantee that they will just go ahead and do the next job on their list, but I also have others who I need to be a bit more watchful of. I have some creative guys that don't do much, but they have the ideas. Some like to be left on their own to create in their own way, whereas others like constant encouragement and appreciation of their efforts. The key is discovering the uniqueness of people and working with it."

Personalisation Hall of Fame...

- **Bill Clinton** — Former president of the United States of America, recognised for making people feel as if they were the only person in the room when he was talking with them.
- **Katharine Cook Briggs** — Astute observer of human behaviour and individual differences who, with her daughter Isabel Briggs Myers, developed the Myers-Briggs Type Indicator ®(MBTI).
- **Carl Gustav Jung** — Swiss psychologist who originated the theory of psychological types, arguing that every person follows their own individual path of personal growth and development.

Personalisation in Relationships — What Works and What to Watch Out For...

Other people feel very appreciated by you because of your ability to see exactly who they are as individuals. The result is that you can relate to a range of people across a range of contexts — so relationships are likely to come naturally to you.

Personalisation at Work — Occupations Where You Could Find a Fit...

- Butler;
- Dentist;
- Judge;
- Psychologist;
- Waiter/Waitress.

Personalisation at Play — Leisure Suggestions You Might Enjoy...

- Correspondence and letter writing;
- Crisis volunteer;
- Mentoring;
- People watching;
- Youth work volunteer.

But Don't Take It Too Far...Personalisation Overplayed...

Don't overpersonalise! Your strength in relating to and valuing each person as a unique individual can, if overplayed, mean that you miss what people have in common. Learn when it may be helpful or appropriate to point out commonalities, or when people need to experience something other than their uniqueness.

Persuasion

People strong in Persuasion are able to bring others round to their way of thinking and to win agreement for what they want to achieve.

If You Have a Strength in Persuasion...

You are extraordinarily effective at convincing others and bringing them around to your point of view. You love to make a good argument for what you want, choosing your language, words and methods carefully, in order to win agreement from others for what you want.

The Persuasion Catchphrase...

"Come on, you know you want to!"

Meet Paul, strong in Persuasion...

"When I would like someone to do something in a different way, it is to some degree making them come to the realisation themselves, so that it becomes their idea and not my idea. Then the best part is that they take ownership of it that way. I had a person on the staff who was used to doing something in a certain way and it was really difficult to get them to look at something really differently. So I said 'Hey, I have been looking at something, take a look at it and see what you think.' He came back in with some questions and I answered them. He came back a few days later and said this is really interesting, and I'm going to do it. Mission accomplished — and all because it had then become his idea."

Persuasion Hall of Fame...

- **Tim Bell** — PR and marketing guru, best known for advising Margaret Thatcher and the Conservative Party through three successful general election campaigns.

- **Karren Brady** — Managing Director of Birmingham City Football Club, which she persuaded David Sullivan to buy and let her run it — in doing so, becoming the first woman to hold the post in the top flight of English football, and the youngest managing director of a UK plc.

- **Og Mandino** — Sales guru and author of *The Greatest Salesman in the World.*

Persuasion in Relationships — What Works and What to Watch Out For...

You have an ability to get others to go along with you. The same traits that make you persuasive also make you attractive to others. You will find that people generally enjoy spending time with you and are willing to let you lead. This gift carries with it a certain responsibility. Be careful not to push others too hard, or to something they don't want, or you will risk breaking their trust in you.

Persuasion at Work — Occupations Where You Could Find a Fit...

- Advertising/marketing executive;
- Advocate;
- Negotiator;
- Politician;
- Salesperson.

Persuasion at Play — Leisure Suggestions You Might Enjoy...

- Blogging;
- Community activist;
- Magic tricks;
- Poker;
- Toastmaster/toastmistress.

But Don't Take It Too Far...Persuasion Overplayed...

Make sure your way is the right way! Your strength in making a good case for what you want and bringing other people round to your way of thinking can, if overplayed, result in you defending or promoting something that you shouldn't. Learn to judge when to step back from deploying your powers of persuasion when, for example, there are more effective or viable alternatives.

Planful

People strong in Planful make plans for everything they do.

If You Have a Strength in Planful...

You have a natural ability to plan and prepare, taking a deliberate and systematic approach to everything you do. Before starting tasks you think carefully, get organised, establish time frames, assess and allocate resources. You love to make sure that you have covered all eventualities — including planning for the unexpected. For you, it's essential to have a plan.

The Planful Catchphrase...

"What's the plan?"

Meet Emma, strong in Planful...

"I just love organising parties and events, it's something that I know that I have been able to do for as long as I can remember. I get a real buzz from bringing people together to have a good time, but I make sure that I plan everything to the very last detail so that everyone really does have a good time. Normally I start to plan well in advance of the event, I plan the venue, who is attending, the food, the entertainment — I even plan to make sure the right people are sitting next to each other so that the party goes with bang. I put a lot of time and effort into the planning stage because I feel that it is the only way that things are guaranteed to go well."

Planful Hall of Fame...

- **Le Corbusier** — Swiss-French architect who designed Chandigarh, the first planned city in India, known internationally for its architecture and urban planning.

- **George Marshall** — Nobel Peace Prize recipient and US Secretary of State; architect of the "Marshall Plan" for the post-war reconstruction of Europe after the Second World War.

- **Marina Raskova** — Soviet aviator who was the first woman to become a navigator in the Soviet Air Force; holder of a number of long distance flight records, for one of which she was decorated with "The Hero of the Soviet Union" award.

Planful in Relationships — What Works and What to Watch Out For...

You love to make plans with other people. You enjoy relationships that are organised and scheduled, with a clear view of what is going to happen when. You are likely to have a harder time with people who are spontaneous or take things as they come, but try to respect their different ways of doing things as they do yours.

Planful at Work — Occupations Where You Could Find a Fit...

- Architect;
- Event organiser;
- Project manager;
- Town planner;
- Wedding planner.

Planful at Play — Leisure Suggestions You Might Enjoy...

- Antique dealing;
- Dinner party hosting;
- Scuba diving;
- Stock market investing;
- Travel.

But Don't Take It Too Far...Planful Overplayed...

Know when to harness spontaneity! Your strength in making plans and taking a systematic approach to everything you do can, if overplayed, mean you will relax only rarely. Learn to spot when a plan is not necessary. Try responding enthusiastically to suggestions to do something spontaneously — you never know, you might even enjoy it!

Prevention

People strong in Prevention think ahead, to anticipate and prevent problems before they happen.

If You Have a Strength in Prevention...

You love to think ahead and anticipate problems before they happen. You notice the little things that might be out of place or going wrong, and then deal with them. You notice, where others may not, areas which need attention to prevent future problems. Your prompt action heads off these future problems, making sure they can't arise in the first place.

The Prevention Catchphrase...

"We can stop that happening if we do this..."

Meet Mark, strong in Prevention...

"Wherever I go, and whatever I do, I am always on the lookout for hidden dangers and pitfalls — and then I like to make sure that I do something so that they don't happen. I walked into my friend's house yesterday. There was a tall wooden door standing propped upright against a cupboard. It had apparently fallen off and was waiting to be fixed. But to me it was just not safe, it could have fallen down at any moment, especially as we had the kids running around. All I could see was that it was an accident waiting to happen. Everything seemed to scream at me to move it. So I quickly put it between two tall cupboards, where it was perfectly safe. I'm the same when I go somewhere and find scissors, medicines, or cables lying around, I just have to move them. If I didn't, I know that they would play on my mind."

Prevention Hall of Fame...

- **Alexander Fleming** — Recipient of the Nobel Prize in Medicine for his discovery of penicillin, which has since been used as an antibiotic in the treatment and prevention of a wide range of infections and illnesses.

- **Kylie Minogue** — Australian actress and pop singer who was diagnosed with breast cancer in 2005; as a result of her openness in speaking about her diagnosis and cancer battle, she encouraged other young women to have regular checks, creating the so-called "Kylie effect".

- **Stella Rimington** — Director-General of MI5, the British Security Service, from 1992—1996; the first woman to hold the post.

Prevention in Relationships — What Works and What to Watch Out For...

You are thoughtful in your relationships, and continually try to anticipate future problems. You are likely to have open discussions about mutual needs or disagreements in an effort to address perceived relationship problems, dealing with them before they turn into major issues. Just remember to go with the flow sometimes, rather than thinking that you have to think everything through from every possible angle.

Prevention at Work — Occupations Where You Could Find a Fit...

- Buildings inspector;
- Health and Safety officer;
- Probation officer;
- Social worker;
- Structural engineer.

Prevention at Play — Leisure Suggestions You Might Enjoy...

- Backgammon/bridge;
- Gardening;
- Social event organiser;
- Volunteer fire officer;
- Youth offender volunteer.

But Don't Take It Too Far...Prevention Overplayed...

Don't forget to live a little! Your strength in thinking ahead and anticipating problems can, if overplayed, hinder your ability to have fun, enjoy yourself, or act spontaneously. Be attuned to when you need to relax your focus. Be prepared to take a risk every now and then — it's good for you and will help to keep you fresh!

Pride

People strong in Pride strive to produce work that is of the highest quality.

If You Have a Strength in Pride...

You take pride in everything that you do. You love consistently to deliver work that is of the highest standard and quality, getting it right first time. You set high standards for yourself, and enjoy the recognition of others for the quality of your work and for what you do.

The Pride Catchphrase...

"Only the best will do."

Meet Tom, strong in Pride...

"I'm not a perfectionist but quality, high quality, is important in everything I suppose. For instance if I am asked to deliver a particular piece of work, I will typically see a way in which the result is exactly what was required, if it is an article, or a report, or whatever, I like to try and create that and make it the best that it can be. I remember that if I cut the grass when I was a child, I'd make sure that every bit was cut. It's about doing a good job, doing the best you can, rather than doing half a job. I think we all have a responsibility to do something well, and people do know that I will give them the best I can give."

Pride Hall of Fame...

- **Judi Dench** — legendary British actress and winner of numerous awards, including ten BAFTAs, seven Laurence Olivier awards and an Academy Award, amongst many others; awarded the OBE and made a Dame Commander of the British Empire for her work.

- **Donatella Versace** — Italian fashion designer and Vice-President of the Versace group, a leading Italian fashion brand.

- **Marco Pierre White** — Youngest British chef to be awarded three Michelin stars and star of the ITV series *Hell's Kitchen* and *Marco's Great British Feast*.

Pride in Relationships — What Works and What to Watch Out For...

You like to receive praise for a job well done and the same holds true for your relationships. Your friends, family members and colleagues who recognise your talents and contributions are the easiest for you to get along with. If the people around you are slovenly in their approach, you're likely to struggle with them.

Pride at Work — Occupations Where You Could Find a Fit...

* Chef;
* Cleaner;
* Fashion designer;
* Interior decorator;
* Jeweller.

Pride at Play — Leisure Suggestions You Might Enjoy...

* Antique car collecting;
* Community clean-up volunteer;
* Cooking;
* Personal exercise and fitness;
* Sudoku.

But Don't Take It Too Far...Pride Overplayed...

Don't be unreasonable! Your strength in setting high standards for yourself and striving to deliver work that is of the highest quality can, if overplayed, make you a harsh critic. Not everyone will take the same pride in their work as you do. That doesn't mean you need to dismiss their contribution. Encourage them, teach them and try to find ways to get the best from them regardless. Everyone has a contribution to make — but they may not always be as top quality as yours!

Rapport Builder

People strong in Rapport Builder establish rapport and relationships with others quickly and easily.

If You Have a Strength in Rapport Builder...

You love to start conversations with people quickly and easily, including people you are meeting for the first time. You quickly find something that is of interest to both of you, and then open up the conversation to establish a relationship. You enjoy meeting people for the first time and quickly get to know them.

The Rapport Builder Catchphrase...

"Very pleased to meet you..."

Meet Jasmine, strong in Rapport Builder...

"I just seem to be able to talk to anybody at any time. I think I even surprised my friend the other day, because she said that she had never seen the man behind the catering counter smile, let alone wave at someone as they were leaving! I am able to talk to receptionists, waiters, taxi drivers, or the chairman of the business. I think what I do is to build a connection with somebody. The starting point of that connection is around engaging with that person in some way, making that person feel comfortable to want to continue with that engagement."

Rapport Builder Hall of Fame...

- **Mo Mowlam** — British Secretary of State for Northern Ireland who oversaw the signing of the historic Good Friday Peace Agreement in 1998, having recovered from a brain tumour.

- **Michael Parkinson** — Legendary British chat show host with his eponymous television show, Parkinson; knighted for his services to broadcasting.

- **Anwar Sadat** — Former president of Egypt and recipient of the Nobel Peace Prize; first leader of an Arab league nation to make a treaty with Israel.

Rapport Builder in Relationships — What Works and What to Watch Out For...

You get along with others and are particularly good at forging new connections. You are great at meeting strangers and are vigilant for common interests and experiences that can bring you together. This makes you perfect for "first contact" situations such as large social gatherings, fundraising and meeting new clients. Be careful that your ability to connect with people does not blind you to the importance of forging deeper relationships that will stand the test of time as well.

Rapport Builder at Work — Occupations Where You Could Find a Fit...

- Bartender;
- Hairdresser;
- Health visitor;
- Receptionist;
- Taxi driver.

Rapport Builder at Play — Leisure Suggestions You Might Enjoy...

- Charity shop volunteer;
- Community event organiser;
- Parent-teacher Association (PTA);
- Socialising;
- Women's group/men's group.

But Don't Take It Too Far...Rapport Builder Overplayed...

Know when to step back! Your strength in building relationships with others quickly and easily can, if overplayed, be perceived by others as inauthentic or intrusive. Not everyone will feel at ease with your desire to connect and build a positive relationship. Some people develop relationships at a slower pace, over time — be sure to give them time to do so, recognising that people are different in how they connect with one another.

Reconfiguration

People strong in Reconfiguration juggle things to meet changing demands and find the best fit for what they want to achieve.

If You Have a Strength in Reconfiguration...

You love rearranging resources and adapting plans to meet the changing demands of new situations. You sense when to stay on track and when to deviate to become more effective. Your adaptability means that you are always looking for the best possible fit for things, always being prepared to change as the context and need changes.

The Reconfiguration Catchphrase...

"We could try it this way...or that way...or this way...or that way..."

Meet Sam, strong in Reconfiguration...

"I just love facilitating large groups. I definitely love it if, on the day, one person was due to speak for an hour and a half, but instead they have spoken for two and a half hours. I have to think quickly and re-arrange things so that we get the best out of the remaining time. I can do that in the moment — absolutely do that in the moment and get a buzz from doing it. I'm always playing with things like this to try and get the best possible result from re-organising and re-arranging them."

Reconfiguration Hall of Fame...

- **Heston Blumenthal** — Chef and owner of the Fat Duck at Bray, renowned as a culinary alchemist for the novel and innovative ways in which he combines foods.

- **Abraham Lincoln** — Former US president who successfully led his country through the American Civil War; signed the Emancipation Proclamation that ended slavery and so changed American society forever.

- **Madonna** — Popular music star; well-known for her ability to change her image and adapt to new social and market conditions.

Reconfiguration in Relationships — What Works and What to Watch Out For...

You are capable of having numerous friendships and juggling your many social responsibilities. You are more likely than others to bounce between groups of friends or form collaborations with different colleagues as circumstances dictate. Be mindful that you don't leave yourself being seen as inauthentic or flighty as a result.

Reconfiguration at Work — Occupations Where You Could Find a Fit...

- Engineer;
- Estate agent;
- Party planner;
- Software developer;
- Town planner.

Reconfiguration at Play — Leisure Suggestions You Might Enjoy...

- Cooking;
- Gardening;
- Home decorating;
- Jigsaws;
- Lego construction.

But Don't Take It Too Far...Reconfiguration Overplayed...

Know when to leave well alone! Your strength in rearranging resources and adapting plans to ensure effective outcomes are achieved can, if overplayed, be exhausting for others. Some people aren't as flexible and adaptable as you. Be attuned to when a more stable and consistent approach will be more successful.

Relationship Deepener

People strong in Relationship Deepener have a natural ability to form deep, long-lasting relationships with people.

If You Have a Strength in Relationship Deepener...

Building close relationships with people is very important to you. For you, really getting to know someone, and for them to know you, takes time. Your relationships with people will develop slowly over time, but nearly always last over the long term.

The Relationship Deepener Catchphrase...

"A friend is a friend for life."

Meet Simon, strong in Relationship Deepener...

"I have made a number of friends over the years and I love keeping in contact with them. I still have close friendships with people I met at when I was at University. Even people that I might not have met for quite a number of years, it is quite a pleasure to get in contact again and meet up. If I am visiting a place where I know I can meet someone from my past, I make sure that I do, even if it is just for a quick coffee. Keeping all my relationships alive is very important to me."

Relationship Deepener Hall of Fame...

- **Athos, Porthos and Aramis** — *The Three Musketeers* of Alexandre Dumas, who live by the motto, "All for one, one for all."

- **Nelson Mandela** — Former President of South Africa; was the key negotiator in bringing an end to the apartheid regime in South Africa, achieved in large part through the relationship he built with white President F. W. De Clerk; both jointly awarded the Nobel Peace Prize as a result.

* **Yang Wan** — Taiwanese woman who has been married to her husband, Liu Yung-yang, for 85 years, making her the longest married woman in the world.

Relationship Deepener in Relationships — What Works and What to Watch Out For...

You are, fundamentally, great in relationships. You connect with others on an intellectual, spiritual, emotional and sometimes physical level. You tend not to have "shallow" or superficial relationships, preferring instead to work to deepen the relationships you have. Be careful not to dismiss connections with others just because they may not immediately go as deep as you might like — people relate in different ways.

Relationship Deepener at Work — Occupations Where You Could Find a Fit...

* Family support worker;
* Foster parent;
* Personal tutor;
* Psychotherapist;
* Pub landlord.

Relationship Deepener at Play — Leisure Suggestions You Might Enjoy...

* Befriending;
* Correspondence and letter writing;
* Dinner party hosting;
* Family time;
* Visiting friends.

But Don't Take It Too Far...Relationship Deepener Overplayed...

Know when to back off! Your strength in building effective, deep, and lasting relationships with people can, if overplayed, mean you direct your efforts inappropriately. Not everyone wants to have the same intensity in their relationships as you do. Learn to gauge when others demand a less intimate approach, or when connecting with someone at a more superficial level will be of mutual benefit. It's okay if every connection you make doesn't necessarily last forever!

Resilience

People strong in Resilience take hardships and setbacks in their stride, recovering quickly and getting on with things again.

If You Have a Strength in Resilience...

You have a terrific ability to overcome adversity. You take hardships and setbacks in your stride with and find the resources and strength to pick yourself back up, even in the most difficult circumstances. You know that you have the strength to cope with, and recover from, anything that life throws at you.

The Resilience Catchphrase...

"You can't keep a good man [or woman] down..."

Meet Nigel, strong in Resilience...

"I have been trying to get my organisation to adopt one particular concept about the way we do things, but the business just wasn't getting it. I kept getting knocked back from it, people just weren't listening, but I kept on track and I didn't let it shake my belief in the whole thing that I was trying to do. I know that the concept is the right way forward and I've just had to be resilient and keep on trying. I keep plugging away, and sometimes you feel like you have it in the palm of your hand, then it goes away and you have to fight back to get it back again. We have made some breakthroughs and these have been pretty significant for me, but really it's only happened because I have kept coping with all of the challenges they have thrown at me and have still been there."

Resilience Hall of Fame...

- **Thomas Edison** — American inventor and holder of 1,093 US patents; most famous as the inventor of the practical electric light bulb — despite having "failed" 1,000 times in his attempts to do so.

- **Helen Keller** — the first deaf and blind woman to earn a college degree; went on to a prolific writing career.

- **Jane Tomlinson** — British amateur athlete who, despite being diagnosed with terminal cancer, raised £1.85 million for charity through a series of athletic challenges, including completing the London Marathon three times, the London Triathlon twice, the New York Marathon once, and cycling across both Europe and the United States.

Resilience in Relationships — What Works and What to Watch Out For...

You tend to be a loyal friend with stable relationships. You are able to recover from interpersonal conflict. At times this means you are forgiving, but mostly it means that you possess a heartiness that helps you to overcome problems with friends, family members and colleagues. People will value you for this — but just be careful that you don't allow them to take advantage of you for it.

Resilience at Work — Occupations Where You Could Find a Fit...

- Ambulance worker;
- Bailiff;
- Consultant;
- Disaster response worker;
- Entrepreneur.

Resilience at Play — Leisure Suggestions You Might Enjoy...

- Dancing;
- Hospice volunteer;
- Mountain climbing;
- Swimming;
- Sailing.

But Don't Take It Too Far...Resilience Overplayed...

Don't become a martyr! Your strength in taking hardships and setbacks in your stride and picking yourself up even in the most difficult circumstances can, if overplayed, become something you take an inappropriate level of pride in. Learn to balance your resilience with an ability to engage as an equal and show humility where necessary.

Resolver

People strong in Resolver love to solve problems, the more difficult the better.

If You Have a Strength in Resolver...

You love solving problems, the more complicated the problem, the better. You thrive on getting your teeth into a really complex problem and focus on getting to the root of it, whatever it might be. You will always go the extra mile to find a solution, being extremely thorough and pursuing all avenues to get a good result. You're never beaten by a problem, but the problems are often beaten by you.

The Resolver Catchphrase...

"Every problem has a solution — and I'll find it."

Meet Harvey, strong in Resolver...

"When I first got this job I was set the challenge of changing our archaic IT and paper-based system and developing an internet system. This may sound trivial now but at the time all the internet projects were failing because people just couldn't make the technology work. The whole thing was a mess but it was a problem that I was well up for. I enjoy solving problems like this. The problem I faced was how could I make this technology work and be secure at the same time. It was a matter of separating the problem into three distinct processes. I worked on the project for 12 months and in the end we had a system that was novel and was adopted by our business and by many other businesses as well."

Resolver Hall of Fame...

- **Archimedes** — Famously cried "Eureka!" when he stepped into a bath and noticed that the water level rose, thereby solving how to calculate the volume of irregular objects, a previously intractable problem.

- **Violeta Chamorro** — Former President of Nicaragua and first elected female head of government in Latin America; her election and policies helped to bring to an end Nicaragua's eleven-year civil war.

- **Marjorie Proops** — English journalist who became the best-known agony aunt in the UK, writing the column *Dear Marje* for the *Daily Mirror*; she was appointed OBE in 1969 and made Woman of the Year in 1984.

Resolver in Relationships — What Works and What to Watch Out For...

Your love of problem solving means that people will like to have you around. Even when your relationships hit problems, you'll be keen to see what you can do to sort them out. Be mindful of when a relationship problem isn't worth solving though, and it might be time to move on.

Resolver at Work — Occupations Where You Could Find a Fit...

- Customer complaints advisor;
- IT engineer;
- Marriage guidance counsellor;
- Plumber;
- Vehicle mechanic.

Resolver at Play — Leisure Suggestions You Might Enjoy...

- Advocacy;
- Car repairing;
- Crossword puzzles;
- Do-it-yourself (DIY);
- Mentoring.

But Don't Take It Too Far...Resolver Overplayed...

Know when to give up! Your strength in tackling problems and persisting to get to the root of problems and sorting things out can, if overplayed, destroy you — maybe not literally, but it will take its toll on your health, well-being and relationships. Learn to spot when a problem cannot be solved. Be prepared to stop when your pursuit of a solution is impacting negatively on other important things in your life — work at keeping perspective on when to persevere and when to withdraw with your efforts at resolution.

Scribe

People strong in Scribe love to write, conveying their thoughts and ideas through the written word.

If You Have a Strength in Scribe...

You love to write, finding a deep fulfilment in playing with words and the joys of written language. You have a natural ability to communicate through writing. The act of writing helps you to clarify your thoughts and you write clearly and easily. You take a positive pleasure in words and love to write things for others to read.

The Scribe Catchphrase...

"I love to write."

Meet Jo, strong in Scribe...

"I was feeling a bit miserable the other day, so I thought that I would cheer myself up by writing a story. So I sat down with my pad and pen and just started to write about the first things that popped into my head. It was a story about persevering through difficulties and helping others, it was set in the jungle and the main characters were all jungle animals. I think I must have spent about 2 hours just solidly writing, but it didn't seem like it. I think I let my imagination run wild as well. I just got lost in the message that I wanted to put across and the words just flowed out. I often write when I'm feeling down, it's a sure fast way of making me smile again."

Scribe Hall of Fame...

- **Jane Austen** — English novelist who wrote in the early nineteenth century, becoming one of the most widely read novelists in English literature, with novels including *Sense and Sensibility* (1811) and *Pride and Prejudice* (1813).

- **William Shakespeare** — English playwright and poet, widely regarded as the greatest writer in the English language; famous for such works as *Romeo and Juliet* and *Hamlet*.

- **Alice Walker** — First black woman winner of the Pulitzer Prize for Fiction, and the National Book Award, both with *The Color Purple* (1982).

Scribe in Relationships — What Works and What to Watch Out For...

You are likely to be a keen observer of human relationships. For you, people are stories and you eagerly take in other people's experiences, emotional reactions and problems. Make sure that other people know that you truly appreciate them, and that they are not simply characters in your life narrative — something which you can do through the way you individualise the messages you write for them in cards, notes and letters.

Scribe at Work — Occupations Where You Could Find a Fit...

- Author;
- Freelancer;
- Journalist;
- Speechwriter;
- Playwright.

Scribe at Play — Leisure Suggestions You Might Enjoy...

- Blogging;
- Crossword puzzles;
- Journaling;
- Letters to the editor;
- Writing.

But Don't Take It Too Far...Scribe Overplayed...

Don't become a bookworm! Your strength in conveying your thoughts and ideas succinctly through writing can, if overplayed, become all-consuming. Balance your love of writing with wider interests, social interaction and fitness activities.

Self-awareness

People strong in Self-awareness know themselves well, understanding their own emotions and behaviour.

If You Have a Strength in Self-awareness...

You enjoy spending time and focusing effort on understanding your behaviour, your emotions, and your responses to different situations. You have a deep awareness and understanding of your strengths and weaknesses. Having this Self-awareness, your behaviour never surprises you or takes you off guard.

The Self-awareness Catchphrase...

"Know thyself."

Meet Rosalind, strong in Self-awareness...

"A constant part of what I do is to arrange for friends to meet up and get together. I think that I would like to spend a lot of energy on that, but I'm very aware that I want to take charge of the whole process, arranging everything down to the last detail — as dotting the I's and crossing the T's is something that I know that I am good at. I'm also aware though, that I can take this too far, and that everybody is a lot happier in the end if they have made some of the arrangements themselves. Recognising this, I have learned to step back and not do so much. So although I make a contribution, I give people a little angle on it themselves. It works better that way, and I've learned to temper what I do so that we get the best result in the end."

Self-awareness Hall of Fame...

- **Kate Adie** — British journalist who is best known for reporting from war zones around the world; her career was launched when she was the first on the scene to report live on the London Iranian Embassy siege in 1980.

- **Bruce Lee** — Chinese American martial artist and actor; considered by many to be the most influential martial artist of the 20th century and a cultural icon.

- **Robert De Niro** — American actor, film director and producer; winner of two Academy Awards; recognised as one of the best actors of his generation for his ability to translate himself into the characters he is playing.

Self-awareness in Relationships — What Works and What to Watch Out For...

You live in a reflective way and know your limits, abilities and preferences very well. Your self-knowledge translates to deeper relationships with others because you are able to grow, change and accept feedback better than most other people. Knowing yourself as you do allows you to be more open to knowing others.

Self-awareness at Work — Occupations Where You Could Find a Fit...

- Actor/actress;
- Drama therapist;
- Group facilitator;
- Negotiator;
- Organisational leader.

Self-awareness at Play — Leisure Suggestions You Might Enjoy...

- Endurance sports;
- Journaling;
- Meditation;
- Reading;
- Yoga.

But Don't Take It Too Far...Self-awareness Overplayed...

Don't become self-obsessed! Your strength in committing time and effort to understanding yourself better can, if overplayed, be perceived as self-indulgent. Balance your focus on yourself with a sufficient focus on others, or on the situation or task at hand.

Service

People strong in Service are constantly looking for ways to serve and help others.

If You Have a Strength in Service...

You feel compelled to help people as much as you can. You get a great deal of satisfaction when you have helped someone. You strive to go above and beyond what you need to do, often exceeding people's expectations. You are focused on satisfying people's needs and meeting their requirements. Nothing is too much trouble.

The Service Catchphrase...

"At your service..."

Meet Teresa, strong in Service...

"A really good day for me is when I have helped a customer. When I have looked into the query that they might have, listened to what they have to say, sorted out the main points, got the information that they require and then got back to that person to give them exactly — and sometimes more than — what they asked for. Yesterday, I had a customer who had been frustrated and distressed by lots of delays. It was one of those really busy days but I took ownership of her case, quickly sorted things with the suppliers and managed to get back to her with some good news the same day. She was really happy with that and actually sent me a thank you card. It was quite rewarding for me, but to be honest, that's what I like to do with everyone that needs help, inside and outside of work — I do what I can, and more, to help them."

Service Hall of Fame...

- **Clara Barton** — American teacher, nurse and humanitarian who is recognised as the organiser of the American Red Cross.

- **Hanuman** — The monkey god from the Indian epic *The Ramayana*, who selflessly serves Rama; sent to fetch sanjivani, a powerful life-restoring herb, from a mountain, Hanuman is unable to find it; legend has it that he then lifts up the entire mountain and returns with it so that others can find the herb.

- **Florence Nightingale** — British nurse most famous for her service during the Crimean War, where she became known as "The Lady with the Lamp" for tending injured soldiers through the night; her book *Notes on Nursing* became the foundation for professional nursing, and International Nurses Day is celebrated around the world on her birthday.

Service in Relationships — What Works and What to Watch Out For...

You view relationships as a chance to help others. You are at your best when you can lend a hand or share your perspective with other people. Make sure to give your service wisely so that you do not get stretched too thin by too many commitments. Also, remember that it is only fair — and right — to ask others for help when you need it, too.

Service at Work — Occupations Where You Could Find a Fit...

- Customer service advisor;
- Dental hygienist;
- Hotelier;
- Nurse;
- Restaurant manager.

Service at Play — Leisure Suggestions You Might Enjoy...

- Befriending;
- Charity shop worker;
- Choir singing;
- Mentoring;
- Volunteering.

But Don't Take It Too Far...Service Overplayed...

Don't be a martyr! Your strength in helping and supporting others on a regular basis and going above and beyond what you need to do can, if overplayed, affect your health and well-being. Avoid becoming so focused on attending to others' needs that you miss meeting your own. You will only be truly able to serve others if your own needs and interests are sufficiently catered for as well.

Spotlight

People strong in Spotlight love to be the focus of everyone's attention.

If You Have a Strength in Spotlight...

You enjoy being the centre of attention. Whether in a meeting or in a social gathering, you naturally speak up and hold the floor. You like holding people's interest and focus, and usually find this easy to do. You find that you can get people to listen to you and keep their attention — whatever else might be going on.

The Spotlight Catchphrase...

"Look at me!"

Meet Sophie, strong in Spotlight...

"Performing is what I am all about. I just love being the centre of everyone's attention and people looking at me, I get a real buzz from doing that. Any opportunity I get, I perform. I like to entertain and to make people laugh, even if it got me into a bit of trouble at school. I think that I have always been like that. As a youngster I was always involved with drama productions, I think that I must have gone to three different drama clubs. And I always wanted to play the lead. I don't do as many drama productions anymore, but even so, I still love to shine. I sing in a band and being on stage in front of all those people really does it for me. Some people get great pleasure from just being associated with something like this and are quite content to stay in the wings. That's not for me though, I want to be up there at the front."

Spotlight Hall of Fame...

- **Shirley Bassey** — Welsh singer who has sold an estimated 135 million records and is the artist with the longest span of Top 40 hits; famous for recording the theme tunes to three James Bond films; regarded as one of the greatest British female artists of all time.

- **Oscar Wilde** — Irish playwright, poet and author of numerous short stories and one novel, who was famous for his biting wit; one of the greatest celebrities of his day.

- **Richard Branson** — British entrepreneur and relentless brand-builder for the Virgin group of companies through his publicity activities and world record attempts, including the fastest crossing of the Atlantic Ocean, by both boat and hot air balloon; the fastest crossing of the Pacific Ocean by hot air balloon; and the fastest crossing of the English Channel in an amphibious vehicle.

Spotlight in Relationships — What Works and What to Watch Out For...

You like to have the attention of other people, so flourish in relationships — as long as other people allow you to by paying you that attention. Beware, though, of hogging the limelight, since other people may need their own time to be noticed as well.

Spotlight at Work — Occupations Where You Could Find a Fit...

- Auctioneer;
- Circus performer;
- Master of Ceremonies;
- Spokesperson;
- TV presenter.

Spotlight at Play — Leisure Suggestions You Might Enjoy...

- Amateur dramatics and theatre;
- Charades;
- Magic tricks;
- Soloist;
- Toastmaster/toastmistress.

But Don't Take It Too Far...Spotlight Overplayed...

Allow others time in the spotlight! Your strength in speaking up and getting others to listen to you can, if overplayed, be at others' expense. Not everyone will be as comfortable being in the spotlight as you are. Make space for, even encourage, others to contribute their thoughts, views and ideas, and reach out to quieter individuals. Inclusion is critical in a team or organisational context. You can certainly hold the floor, but allow others their opportunity too!

Strategic Awareness

People strong in Strategic Awareness pay attention to the wider factors and the bigger picture that will inform the decisions they make to achieve their objectives.

If You Have a Strength in Strategic Awareness...

You have a keen interest in understanding changes in the wider world that could impact on your plans and objectives. This big picture awareness enables you to develop and shift long-term plans effectively, and from this you love to take steps to deal with whatever circumstances may arise in the future.

The Strategic Awareness Catchphrase...

"Look at this...what does it mean for us?"

Meet Alan, strong in Strategic Awareness...

"I'm always looking up and out across the horizon — both figuratively and literally. I love to think about what the future will bring, and often when I'm doing that, I stare out over the horizon and try to picture what might be coming. I watch the news, read informed comments, study the industry journals, track trends, pay attention to anomalies, and then try and compute all of that information, pulling it all together so that I have a view on what's going to happen next and what it means for me and for the company. We didn't predict the credit crunch coming exactly, but we did know that things were going to get more difficult, and we spotted it sooner than a lot of other people. As a result, we put plans in place to deal with it, and that has helped us a lot. Even now, as we're working through this, I'm still always looking over that horizon, seeing what is going to come next. Not only is that my job as the CEO, it's what I love to do."

Strategic Awareness Hall of Fame...

- **Catherine II (the Great)** — Empress of Russia from 1762 until 1796; under her rule Russia was revitalised through a number of complex foreign policy successes and improved administration.
- **Marjorie Scardino** — First female Chief Executive of a FTSE-100 company when she was made CEO of Pearson in 1997; recognised for her strategic awareness and business acumen.
- **Sun Tzu** — Chinese philosopher born in the sixth century BC; served as a general to the King of Wu, wrote *The Art of War* on the basis of his military successes.

Strategic Awareness in Relationships — What Works and What to Watch Out For...

You have a very broad view of relationships and can often consider situational or circumstantial factors that impact decisions and conflict. This makes you adept at dealing with problems and not getting drawn into petty squabbles, preferring instead to look at the larger picture of your relationships overall.

Strategic Awareness at Work — Occupations Where You Could Find a Fit...

- Art dealer;
- Financial advisor;
- Military commander;
- Product designer;
- Stockbroker.

Strategic Awareness at Play — Leisure Suggestions You Might Enjoy...

- Antiques dealing;
- Chess;
- Computer football manager;
- Pinochle (card game);
- Stock market investment.

But Don't Take It Too Far...Strategic Awareness Overplayed...

Don't over-strategise! Your strength can, if overplayed, result in practical realities being ignored. Spot when the shift needs to be made from strategy and the "big picture" to the nitty-gritty of planning, detail and practicalities. Strategic thinking is just day-dreaming when it doesn't lead to action.

Time
Optimiser

*People strong in Time Optimiser maximise
their time to get the most out of whatever
time they have available in whatever situation.*

If You Have a Strength in Time Optimiser...

Time is very precious to you and you never waste it. You love to squeeze as much as you can into every minute of each day, organising yourself so that you use your time wisely and productively. Whatever situation you are in, you are making the most of your time.

The Time Optimiser Catchphrase...

"What can I be doing at this moment to make the best use of my time?"

Meet Jared, strong in Time Optimiser...

"I just hate waiting around. Some experiments that I do involve adding A to B, and then to C, and then waiting on them for fairly long periods of time. Well, to me, 5 minutes seems interminable. I just can't stand the waiting, I just find it so frustrating sitting there waiting for the next thing to have to happen. I hate it when I watch others do the same thing, it seems such a waste of time. So I have devised a whole new protocol for the way these experiments work. It involves a lot of planning and preparation beforehand, but it essentially means that we can run 5 experiments at the same time, and the time that it saves in the long run is monumental. Just think — we used to do 5 experiments in 5 days — and now we do 25. Brilliant!"

Time Optimiser Hall of Fame...

- **Adrian Furnham** — Professor of Psychology at University College London, most prolific and published European academic psychologist.

- **Lillian Gilbreth** — Industrial engineer, industrial psychologist, university professor, author, consultant, first woman elected into the National Academy of Engineering — and mother to twelve children. What more can we say?!

- **Ruth Lawrence** — Gained an O-level in Mathematics at the age of nine years; admitted to St. Hugh's College, University of Oxford, at the age of twelve years.

Time Optimiser in Relationships — What Works and What to Watch Out For...

You are conscious of how you spend your time. You are likely to have relationships that are scheduled and to engage in events that are planned well in advance. To stretch yourself, try letting more spontaneous friends set the agenda and enjoy the lack of structure that results — resisting the need to feel that you have to cram everything into every moment.

Time Optimiser at Work — Occupations Where You Could Find a Fit...

- Bomb disposal expert;
- Chef;
- Contractor;
- Postal worker;
- Project manager.

Time Optimiser at Play — Leisure Suggestions You Might Enjoy...

- Cooking;
- Distance running;
- Photography;
- Scuba diving;
- Timed chess.

But Don't Take It Too Far...Time Optimiser Overplayed...

Don't optimise every second! Your strength in organising your life to maximise your use of time can, if overplayed, be exhausting for others and eventually yourself. Some people aren't as time-conscious as you. Learn to enjoy moments when you aren't rushing somewhere, doing something, or achieving anything in particular. Sometimes the best way to spend your time is in doing nothing!

Unconditionality

WELCOME

People strong in Unconditionality accept people for who and what they are, without ever needing to judge them.

If You Have a Strength in Unconditionality...

You have an immense capacity to accept people genuinely for who they are, without ever judging them. You watch and accept people with respect, for you believe that everyone is valuable in their own right. No matter what people may have done — you accept everyone the same: unconditionally.

The Unconditionality Catchphrase...

"I value and accept you for being you."

Meet Helen, strong in Unconditionality...

"We're a close group of friends, we all met at university and most of the time we get on very well. However, just recently one of my friends did something that upset the rest of the group and actually caused quite a rift amongst us all. Everyone was talking and gossiping about her and the strong emails were flying thick and fast. I felt really uncomfortable, I never like being associated with gossiping and judging people like that. I wanted to understand why she had behaved in the way she had, because I am sure that she had a reason for why she did what she did. I kept finding myself defending her actions because I really didn't think that people should have judged her like they did. After all, we've all made mistakes, and it's important to accept people whatever they have done."

Unconditionality Hall of Fame...

- **Mata Amritanandamayi** — Indian Hindu spiritual leader known as the "Hugging Saint" and widely respected for her humanitarian activities.

- **Jerold Bozarth** — Leading practitioner of non-directive client-centred therapy, of which unconditional positive regard is one of the central precepts.

- **Mother Teresa of Calcutta** — Albanian Catholic nun and founder of the Missionaries of Charity, in Calcutta, India; Nobel Peace Prize recipient for her humanitarian work.

Unconditionality in Relationships — What Works and What to Watch Out For...

You are extraordinarily accepting of others. You can truly accept their faults as well as their good qualities. This makes you a loyal, dependable friend and colleague and you likely have many deep relationships. Other people appreciate and trust you. Take care, though, that your acceptance of others does not leave you open to them taking advantage of you. Acceptance needs to be coupled with a respect that is reciprocated.

Unconditionality at Work — Occupations Where You Could Find a Fit...

- Counsellor;
- Mediator;
- Probation officer;
- Stay-at-home parent;
- Youth worker.

Unconditionality at Play — Leisure Suggestions You Might Enjoy...

- Befriender;
- Family time;
- Visiting friends;
- Working in a soup kitchen;
- Youth offender volunteer.

But Don't Take It Too Far...Unconditionality Overplayed...

Don't be too forgiving! Your strength in appreciating and accepting people for who they are can, if overplayed, make you blind to behaviour that is unacceptable. Balance your acceptance of others with a willingness to be an honest friend when required. Tough love is sometimes the best course of action, even if you would rather always assume the best of everyone.

Work Ethic

> People strong in Work Ethic are very hard workers, putting a lot of effort into everything they do.

If You Have a Strength in Work Ethic...

You are an extremely hard worker, putting a lot of effort and energy into your work. You enjoy putting in extra hours and are capable of working longer — and over a longer period of time — than most other people. You are aware that you work much harder than others, and you enjoy doing so.

The Work Ethic Catchphrase...

"You only get out what you put in."

Meet Peter, strong in Work Ethic...

"I always work hard. I remember as a child that I would come home on a Friday and the first thing I would want to do is to get all my homework done. It wasn't just so that I could get it out of the way, but more that I had the whole weekend to devote to it and I could do it properly. I'm the same now, I love being busy and although I'm at home with the children, I fill my day with lots of things to do. Last week was a good example of how I like to keep myself busy, as if I hadn't got enough to do already! So besides all the normal things, like preparing the children's lunches, doing the washing, ironing, and cleaning, I took on the task of painting the outside of our house. It was something that I really looked forward to doing. I knew that it wasn't going to be easy, but I was ready to put the effort in."

Work Ethic Hall of Fame...

- **John Henry** — Figure in American folklore; known for his hard work on railroads and for having raced against a steam-powered hammer in a competition, and won, only to die in victory.

- **Mary Robinson** — First female President of Ireland and Chair of the Council of Women World Leaders, amongst numerous other positions.

- **Queen Victoria** — Served as Queen of the United Kingdom of Great Britain and Ireland for 63 years and 7 months, the longest reign of any female monarch in history and longer than any other British monarch before or since.

Work Ethic in Relationships — What Works and What to Watch Out For...

You naturally throw yourself into your work, so it is especially important that you take time out to balance your work life with your family and social life. This means scheduling time for friends, family, learning and relaxation. It is typically easy for you to win the respect of colleagues because of your work ethic. You may need to be mindful of making sure that you also put as much effort into your social and family relationships, and into how you look after yourself.

Work Ethic at Work — Occupations Where You Could Find a Fit...

- Coal miner;
- Doctor;
- Lawyer;
- Taxi driver;
- Tradesperson (e.g., carpenter, electrician, plumber).

Work Ethic at Play — Leisure Suggestions You Might Enjoy...

- Bicycling;
- Mountain climbing;
- Relaxing;
- River swimming;
- Water polo.

But Don't Take It Too Far...Work Ethic Overplayed...

Know when enough is enough! Your strength in working hard and doing more than is expected of you can, if overplayed, have a negative impact on your health, well-being and relationships. Listen to what others tell you and strive for a balance that meets your wider life needs, not just those of work. Be careful also not to judge others according to your own strong work ethic — the right balance will be unique to each person.

Strengths Symbology

"A picture is worth a thousand words"

Anon.

Throughout recorded history, symbols have been used as a communication media that transcends language, history and culture. Symbols speak to the deeper truth of something that is not easily rendered in words. They are as old as humankind itself.

In the modern age, symbols continue to be all around us. We recognise them as the badges and insignia of group membership — whether sports teams, political parties, or other groups; whether road user information; or whether corporate brands and logos. Media advertising is replete with symbols, as marketers use symbolic associations in the effort to position their brands and products in our minds alongside the desired attributes created by the symbols.

Generally speaking, symbols are used to emphasise the positive rather than the negative: virtue not vice; hope not despair; strength not weakness. It is only fitting, therefore, that we have developed a strengths symbology for Realise2, to honour the wisdom of the ages in creating a deeper understanding of, and resonance with, human strengths.

A symbology may refer to the *study* of the symbols, the *use* of the symbols, or the symbols themselves *collectively*. Our strengths symbology is all three, since it is concerned with understanding how the symbols represent the different strengths, how they are used, and the symbols collectively.

In the entries that follow, we introduce you to the symbols that we have chosen to represent each of the 60 strengths in Realise2. Welcome to the Realise2 strengths symbology.

Symbols Bibliography

Cooper, J. C. (1979). *An illustrated encyclopaedia of traditional symbols*. London: Thames & Hudson.

Fontana, D. (1997). *The secret language of symbols: A visual key to symbols and their meanings*. London: Piatkus.

Tresidder, J. (2003). *1001 symbols: The illustrated key to the world of symbols*. London: Duncan Baird Publishers.

Realise2 Strengths Symbology

 Action — The clapperboard is used in film making to highlight the "Action" of the famous movie-making phrase, "Lights, Camera, Action!"

 Adherence — The check list being ticked off is one way in which people can ensure that they are doing everything they are supposed to do.

 Adventure — People strong in Adventure take risks and stretch themselves, just like the mountaineer in this strengths symbol.

 Authenticity — The wax seal has been used throughout the ages to show that important documents were the authentic originals, and not a copy that had been altered by someone else.

 Bounceback — People with Bounceback use setbacks as a springboard to go on and do even better.

 Catalyst — Catalysts make things happen, and in this strengths symbol, the match provides the spark for things to start.

 Centred — The dot at the centre of the circle is one of the oldest symbols in symbology, and was often taken to represent the sun.

 Change Agent — The Greek symbol delta, here represented by a triangle, is a universal symbol for change.

 Compassion — People strong in Compassion care about others, as this universally-recognised symbol suggests.

 Competitive — The trophy symbolises victory, which is what everyone with a Competitive strength will be striving for — to win.

 Connector — People strong in Connector are always at the hub of the people they have connected.

 Counterpoint — Like this fish swimming against the flow, people with Counterpoint will always bring a different perspective.

 Courage — The lion symbolises Courage throughout many histories and cultures.

Creativity — The artist's palette and paint brush is the archetypal modern symbol for Creativity, but still represents only one of the ways in which Creativity may be made manifest.

 Curiosity — Curiosity is all about asking questions, as this strengths symbol suggests.

 Detail — The strength of Detail is about looking into the minutiae, which this microscope is used to convey.

 Drive — People strong in Drive have a distinct energy about them, captured here by the lightning bolt of the strengths symbol.

 Efficacy — Efficacy represents a confidence about being successful, as this thought bubble of achievement shows.

 Emotional Awareness — The thermometer within the heart symbolises how people strong in Emotional Awareness are sensitive to the needs and emotions of others.

 Empathic Connection — Two hands joining in the shape of a heart are used for Empathic Connection, when people are connected through their shared understanding of what the other is feeling.

 Enabler — The seed grows in this person's hand, symbolising the role that they play as an Enabler, creating the conditions for other people to learn how to do things for themselves.

 Equality — The ruler (or rule) is used to measure, and in the case of the person strong in Equality, to measure and ensure that all receive equal parts.

 Esteem Builder — Esteem Builders are amazing at finding the beauty and capability that lies within, like the pearl within this oyster shell.

 Explainer — They might not always need chalk and a blackboard, but these symbols are typical of the tools of an Explainer.

 Feedback — Feedback is a two-way process, so this arrows show the flow of dialogue through the feedback process.

Gratitude — Flowers can be a wonderful way to say thank you and show appreciation, so they became the Gratitude strengths symbol.

Growth — The acorn is an archetypal symbol of growth and development, since from small acorns large oak trees grow.

 Humility — The humble bumble bee works only to serve his or her queen, and so becomes our strengths symbol for Humility.

 Humour — The laughing face is a universal symbol for Humour, and so we use it here as the strengths symbol.

 Improver — People strong in Improver always want to make things better, symbolised here by the pencil being sharpened.

 Incubator — The thought bubble shows where Incubators spend their time — thinking things through as they ponder and reflect.

 Innovation — Represented here by chemical experimentation, the symbol for Innovation represents trying things out in different and original ways.

 Judgement — To ensure the right decision, people strong in Judgement will weigh the evidence and options on all sides, as these scales show.

 Legacy — People strong in Legacy want to leave things that will outlast them, symbolised here by the longevity of the tree.

 Listener — The human ear is an archetypal symbol for listening.

 Mission — This rocket ship is shooting for the stars, and symbolises how people strong in Mission will always be heading straight for what is important to them.

 Moral Compass — The compass here helps people to guide their decisions against the true north of what is the ethical and right thing to do.

 Narrator — The story book symbolises what the Narrator loves to do — tell stories!

 Optimism — Is the glass half-full or half-empty? This well-recognised way of asking whether someone is an optimist or a pessimist is used here as the strengths symbol for Optimism.

 Order — People strong in Order will have a place for everything, as the neat arrangement of this bookshelf suggests.

Persistence — Like the tortoise who won his race against the hare, people strong in Persistence will just keep going until they get there in the end.

 Personal Responsibility — When people strong in Personal Responsibility commit to do something, they hold themselves accountable for doing it, symbolised here by the "hand on the heart" of a solemn promise.

 Personalisation — People strong in Personalisation are acutely interested in you, symbolised here by the abbreviation "U" on the signet ring.

 Persuasion — The lyre is renowned throughout mythology as playing the sweet music that allows people to bring others around to their way of thinking.

 Planful — Diaries and calendars are a very good way of knowing what you are going to be doing and when, as this strengths symbol for Planful conveys.

 Prevention — The lighthouse is well-recognised in its role of preventing disaster by warning ships to steer clear of the rocks.

 Pride — The "Quality Assured" stamp says it all about Pride — people with this strength will always strive to produce work that is of the highest quality.

 Rapport Builder — The handshake (and its cultural variants) are universally recognised symbols of greeting, well-used by people strong in Rapport Builder.

 Reconfiguration — People strong in Reconfiguration see life as a jigsaw puzzle, and are always looking for the best fit of what will go where.

 Relationship Deepener — The diamond wedding anniversary is achieved after only 60 years of marriage, making it a fitting strengths symbol for Relationship Deepener.

 Resilience — The shield symbolises the strength of Resilience, and how it enables people to keep challenges, setbacks and disappointments at bay.

 Resolver — The Swiss Army knife seems to have a function for every situation, and so is used here to symbolise the strength of Resolver.

Scribe — People strong in Scribe love to write, as is conveyed by this strengths symbol.

 Self-awareness — The hand mirror is used to symbolise the strength of Self-awareness, whereby people know themselves well, understanding their emotions and motivations.

 Service — The waiter is renowned for his Service, but people strong in Service will use their strength to help and serve others in any different number of ways.

 Spotlight — The spotlight is what is sought by people with this strength, so the strengths symbol provides it for them.

 Strategic Awareness — Always looking out over the horizon to see what might be coming next, aware of the different factors that could impact upon them, the telescope symbolises Strategic Awareness.

 Time Optimiser — The clock symbolises time, and this is the unique focus of the Time Optimiser — how to make the most of whatever time is available in whatever situation.

 Unconditionality — For people strong in Unconditionality, everyone is welcome, no matter who they are or what they have done.

 Work Ethic — The ox is universally revered for its capacity for work, and so is used here as the strengths symbol for Work Ethic.

Appendix 1

Strengths: The Scientific Source Material

In Strengths: The Evidence we gave you ten benefits of using your strengths more. Here is the original scientific source material from which those conclusions were drawn.

1. People who use their strengths more are happier:

Govindji and Linley (2007), in a study of 214 university students, showed that people who used their strengths more reported higher levels of subjective well-being (i.e., happiness) and psychological well-being (i.e., fulfilment). Similarly, Proctor, Maltby and Linley (2009) reported similar findings with a study of 135 university students. Seligman, Steen, Park and Peterson (2005) found that people who used their strengths in a new and different way every day reported higher levels of happiness and lower levels of depression, and this lasted over time. Minhas (2010) showed that people who developed their realised or unrealised strengths reported higher levels of happiness and well-being over a four-week period. Park, Peterson and Seligman (2004) found that people who reported higher levels of character strengths also reported higher levels of life satisfaction, especially for so-called "strengths of the heart".

2. People who use their strengths more are more confident:

Govindji and Linley (2007) found that people who used their strengths more reported higher levels of self-efficacy, which is a scientific conception of confidence — the belief that we are capable of achieving the things we want to achieve. This finding was replicated by Proctor, Maltby and Linley (2009) in a study with 135 university students.

3. People who use their strengths more have higher levels of self-esteem:

Minhas (2010) found that people who developed their realised or unrealised strengths reported increases in self-esteem over a four-week period. Govindji and Linley (2007) reported that people who used their strengths more reported higher levels of self-esteem. In a study with 135 university students, Proctor, Maltby and Linley (2009) found that strengths use was associated with higher levels of self-esteem.

4. People who use their strengths more have higher levels of energy and vitality:

Govindji and Linley (2007), in a study with 214 university students, found that strengths use was associated with higher levels of psychological vitality, that is, having feelings of positive energy and buzz.

5. People who use their strengths more experience less stress:

Over a six-month time period with a community sample of 207 people, those people who used their strengths more reported lower levels of stress. This was the case at both the baseline period, where strengths use was associated with less stress, and also over the three-month and six-month follow ups, where higher strengths use predicted lower stress over time (Wood, Linley, Maltby, & Hurling, 2010).

6. People who use their strengths more are more resilient:

Analysis of the Ego Resiliency Scale with Realise2 shows that strengths use is associated with higher levels of resilience for fifty of the sixty Realise2 strengths (CAPP, 2010). The two highest correlations were with Resilience (as you might expect) and Adventure, which suggests that stretching yourself outside of your comfort zone can be a way to build your resilience. The ten strengths where higher strengths use was *not* significantly associated with higher resilience were Adherence, Competitive, Detail, Humour, Order, Planful, Prevention, Scribe, Time Optimiser, and Work Ethic.

7. People who use their strengths more are more likely to achieve their goals:

Linley, Nielsen, Wood, Gillett and Biswas-Diener (2010) showed that people who used their strengths in striving to achieve their goals were far more likely to achieve those goals. When they achieved their goals, they satisfied their psychological needs and were happier and more fulfilled as a result.

8. People who use their strengths more perform better at work:

In a study of 19,187 employees from 34 organisations across seven industries and 29 countries, the Corporate Leadership Council (2002) found that when managers emphasised performance strengths, performance was 36.4% higher, and when they emphasised personality strengths, performance was 21.3% higher. In contrast, emphasising weaknesses led to a 26.8% decline for performance weaknesses and a 5.5% decline for personality weaknesses. Data from our own work with Norwich Union shows that people working from their strengths perform better and stay with the company longer (Stefanyszyn, 2007).

9. People who use their strengths more are more engaged at work:

The opportunity to do what you do best each day, that is, using our strengths, is a core predictor of workplace engagement, which in turn is a core predictor of a range of business outcomes (Harter, Schmidt, & Hayes, 2002). Similarly, Minhas (2010) found that work engagement increased when people developed either their realised or unrealised strengths.

10. People who use their strengths more are more effective at developing themselves and growing as individuals:

When focusing on self-development, people improve faster on areas where they are already strong, than they do in areas where they are weak, contrary to some popular perceptions that focusing on weakness development brings the greatest return (Sheldon, Kasser, Smith & Share, 2002). Case study evidence from our own work on leadership development with BAE Systems showed that business leaders who focused on developing themselves and their teams on the basis of their strengths were more effective and successful (Smedley, 2007).

References

CAPP (2010). *Technical manual and statistical properties for Realise2*. Coventry, UK: CAPP.

Corporate Leadership Council (2002). *Performance management survey*. Washington, DC: Author.

Govindji, R., & Linley, P. A. (2007). Strengths use, self-concordance and well-being: Implications for strengths coaching and coaching psychologists. *International Coaching Psychology Review, 2* (2), 143–153.

Harter, J. K., Schmidt, F. L., & Hayes, T. L. (2002). Business-unit-level relationship between employee satisfaction, employee engagement, and business outcomes: A meta-analysis. *Journal of Applied Psychology, 87,* 268–279.

Linley, P. A., Nielsen, K. M., Wood, A. M., Gillett, R., & Biswas-Diener, R., (2010). Using signature strengths in pursuit of goals: Effects on goal progress, need satisfaction, and well-being, and implications for coaching psychologists. *International Coaching Psychology Review, 5* (1), 8–17.

Minhas, G. (2010). Developing realised and unrealised strengths: Implications for engagement, self-esteem, life satisfaction and well-being. *Assessment and Development Matters,* in press.

Park, N., Peterson, C., & Seligman, M. E. P. (2004). Strengths of character and well-being. *Journal of Social and Clinical Psychology, 23,* 603–619.

Proctor, C., Maltby, J., & Linley, P. A. (2009) Strengths use as a predictor of well-being and health- related quality of life. *Journal of Happiness Studies, 10,* 583–630.

Seligman, M. E. P., Steen, T. A., Park, N., & Peterson, C. (2005). Positive psychology progress: Empirical validation of interventions. *American Psychologist, 60,* 410–421.

Sheldon, K. M., Kasser, T., Smith, K., & Share, T. (2002). Personal goals and psychological growth: Testing an intervention to enhance goal-attainment and personality integration. *Journal of Personality, 70,* 5–31.

Smedley, T. (2007, 1 November). The powers that BAE. *People Management,* 40–42.

Stefanyszyn, K. (2007). Norwich Union changes focus from competencies to strengths, *Strategic HR Review, 7,* 10–11.

Wood, A. M., Linley, P. A., Maltby, J., & Hurling, R. (2010). Use of positive psychological strengths leads to less stress and greater self-esteem, vitality, and positive affect over time: A three-wave longitudinal study and validation of the Strengths Use Scale. *Manuscript submitted for publication.*

Appendix 2

Sample Realise2 Personal Development Plan

Visit **www.strengths2020.com** to download a blank Personal Development Plan for your own use.

Name: Simon Lester
Date: 05/11/2009

	Activity	Barriers
	What do you want to develop — and what are you going to do?	*What is likely to prevent you from developing this strength? What might hinder progress?*
Realised Strengths		
Explainer	To build on my strengths in being able to explain plans and processes to people — and to extend this to explain to people about how I want to see them perform and develop.	Time pressures that are focused on day-to-day delivery, rather than longer term people development. I will overcome these by making sure I schedule time for these conversations and sticking to that time.
Unrealised Strengths		
Feedback	To improve my ability to give feedback to my team and to develop them as individuals.	My mental models of feedback and that it is difficult to give, despite the fact I am very effective at doing it with the under-12s football coaching.

Enablers	Support	Milestones
What is prompting or pushing you to develop this strength? What will the benefits be?	*Who will help you develop — whose support do you need?*	*What are the key milestones that will help you reach your goal?*
I have recently been promoted and I need to raise my game on delivering performance through others. I have decided to draw on the strengths I already have as a way of doing so, and Explainer is one of my strengths. The benefits will be better team and business performance.	I will need to practice explaining things that are more outside of my comfort zone. As daft as it might sound, I will practice on my kids — explaining to them what I want them to do and why.	Day-to-day, I will have more conversations with people where I am explaining what I want from them and why I want it. I will monitor weekly how many conversations I have had that are not just about explaining plans and processes, but also more people-focused.
I need to improve my team performance scores for my 360-degree review feedback. Getting better at enabling people to do things for themselves will also help my teams perform better and support the business performance.	I have a couple of key confidantes on my team who can help me: Richard and Jo. They have both agreed to let me practice on them and to work with me to improve my feedback.	Delivering a far more successful performance review season for my team, as well as giving more real-time feedback on an ongoing basis. Both should be reflected in my 360-degree review feedback scores.

Acknowledgements

We would like to thank our CAPP colleagues, present and past, who have contributed their strengths to the development of CAPP, Realise2 and *The Strengths Book*: Tony Andrews, Avirupa Bhaduri, Dominic Carter, Jenny Fox Eades, Reena Govindji, Sue Harrington, Jonathan Hill, Desmond O'Dowd, Debasish "Micky" Sen Sharma, Doug Lapsley, Gurpal Minhas, Kissa Faith Mwenelupembe, and Linda Woolston. We thank especially Emma Trenier and Trudy Bailey for their consistent input, feedback, and support to the development of *The Strengths Book*. We needed it!

Collectively, the Author Team

I would like to thank the people who have given me the strength to strengthen others, educating me about strengths through our conversations or through the legacy they left through their writings and through others: Aristotle, Bernard Haldane, Bob Kaplan, Christopher Peterson, Donald Clifton, Dr. William E. Hall, Jim Meehan, Jonathan Hill, Marty Seligman, Mike Pegg, Peter Drucker, Rob Kaiser, Robert Sternberg. To David Taylor, thank you for the Warwick Business School lunch conversation that unlocked me. To Seth Godin, thank you for *Linchpin* which helped me defeat the resistance. To Malcolm Gladwell, thank you for the lessons of *What the Dog Saw*, which helped me improve my craft. And finally, as always, I thank my family for allowing me to become who I am: my mother and father, my wife, Jenny, and our four children, Jack, Lucy, Sophie and Ben. You are my legacy.

Alex Linley

Over the years my eyes and ears have been opened to strengths both within myself and others by many people, including Donald Clifton, Jonathan Hill, Bill Tallon, Alex Linley and Nicky Garcea. To these colleagues and friends, I would like to express my sincere thanks. I am also truly indebted to the many thousands of people who have shared their personal stories with me; you have given so much and I have loved listening to you. Every conversation has been unique; thank you for allowing me into parts of your life to uncover your strengths, so that I can share these wonderful characteristics with others. Last but not least, thank you to my family, who, although we share the same genes, show that everyone is different and that each person has a unique combination of strengths, which set them apart from others: to my mum and dad, my husband, Gary, and our children, Robert, Beth and Hannah. I love you.

Janet Willars

I would like to thank Don Clifton, Chris Peterson, Marty Seligman and Neal Mayerson; all of whom have influenced my thinking about strengths. I would also like to thank my wife, Keya, for all her support. Finally, I would like to thank the people of Shiritri in Kolkata, India, for their many inspirational examples of strengths even in the face of dire poverty.

Robert Biswas-Diener

I would like to thank the people who have influenced my view and practice of business psychology: Alex Linley, Barbara Fredrickson, Jean Twenge, Jonathan Hill and Martin Seligman. To Alex for his capacity to continually spot and nurture strengths in others and to the rest of the CAPP team. We have collectively created a unique strengths-based organisation and each of you has made this book come to light through your desire to innovate, narrate, scribe and work unbelievably hard. Lastly, thank you to my family, Mum for your optimism, Dad for your authenticity, and Nick for your love and perspective.

Nicky Garcea

First, my thanks go to my CAPP colleagues for their invitation to join them on the journey that has been Realise2. It is a pleasure and privilege to work with you. Second, I must thank the many colleagues, employees, children and parents that I have spoken to and worked with in a professional context over the past 20 years, who have enlightened me to the full diversity that is human nature and human strengths. You are my lifelong education. Third, I thank my family — my parents, my brother, Tony, for your enduring love and friendship, which are most definitely your greatest strengths. Fourth, to Candy my wife, thank you for sharing your strengths with me and for embracing, and tolerating, mine! Finally, to our children — William, Josephine and Daniel — may you find your own pathways to understanding and realising the unique strengths that you each possess, and may this book contribute in some small way to helping you along on that journey.

Martin Stairs

About the authors

Dr. Alex Linley is a world authority on positive psychology and its applications, particularly strengths approaches. He is the Founding Director of the Centre of Applied Positive Psychology and Visiting Professor in Psychology at the University of Leicester, UK. Through his consulting work, he applies strengths to people management practices across the employee life cycle with organisations spanning the public and private sectors. He has written, co-written, or edited more than 130 research papers and book chapters, and six books, including *Positive Psychology in Practice* (Wiley, 2004), *Average to A+: Realising Strengths in Yourself and Others* (CAPP Press, 2008) and the *Oxford Handbook of Positive Psychology and Work* (Oxford University Press, 2009). Alex has served as Associate Editor of the *Journal of Positive Psychology* and the *Encyclopedia of Positive Psychology* (Blackwell, 2009), and is currently Co-Editor of the *International Coaching Psychology Review*.

Dr. Janet Willars passionately enjoys discovering the talents and strengths of individuals, positioning them for success and allowing them the opportunities to use their talents both in and outside of the workplace every day. Janet has been involved in the work of strengths-based organisations for the last 15 years and has a wealth of experience in developing, conducting and analysing strengths-based interviews. She has interviewed approximately 23,000 people, discovering strengths for the financial services sector, and both the service and retail industries. Janet also has experience of interview-based qualitative research in industrial settings. Her work at CAPP focuses on "in-depth" assessments of individuals to uncover and understand their strengths; facilitating focus groups to identify the key strengths of talented individuals; developing interview strategies to allow the recruitment and retention of talent; and, training courses to facilitate a wider understanding of strengths and strengths-based interviews.

Dr. Robert Biswas-Diener is widely known as the "Indiana Jones of Positive Psychology" because his research on strengths and well-being has taken him to such far-flung destinations as Greenland, India and Kenya. He has published more than two dozen scientific articles and chapters on strengths and happiness. Robert is a Certified Mentor Coach and is Programme Director for Education & Learning at CAPP.

He is author of *Positive Psychology Coaching* (2007) and *Happiness: Unlocking the Mysteries of Psychological Wealth* (2008), which won the 2008 PROSE Award for Psychology, for excellence in academic publishing. He lives in Portland, Oregon (USA).

Nicky Garcea is a Chartered Occupational Psychologist and Consulting Director at the Centre of Applied Positive Psychology (CAPP). Nicky's area of research and consulting expertise span recruitment, development and performance management. She has designed and delivered consulting assignments for a range of private and public sector clients in the UK, Nigeria, Argentina, Venezuela, the United States and Canada. In recent years she has led a team of psychologists at CAPP to deliver pioneering organisational projects that integrate positive psychology and best practice occupational psychology. Nicky has published her work in a variety of journals including *HR Director, PersonalFuhrung* and *Selection and Development Review*. She has also edited a special issue of *Organisations and People* on "Applying Positive Psychology in Organisations" and is a regular speaker at HR and occupational psychology events.

Martin Stairs is a Chartered Occupational Psychologist and specialist in occupational assessment, leadership development, and employee engagement. Throughout his consultancy career he has worked extensively with public sector clients and leading blue-chip organisations across the UK and Europe, as well as internationally in Asia, the US and Australia. He has led the design of a wide range of leadership development and talent management programmes, and continues to provide his expertise as a coach and assessor to a broad client base. Martin is a member of the British Psychological Society and an Affiliate Member of the Chartered Institute of Personnel and Development (CIPD). He holds a Masters degree in Occupational Psychology, as well as first degrees in Psychology and Physics. He is a qualified teacher and previously worked in the NHS and with a children's charity dedicated to providing care, education and therapy to traumatised children and young people. Martin is based in rural Oxfordshire where he lives with his wife and family.

Where Next?

1. **Now you know about strengths, do you want to find out about your *own* strengths, weaknesses and learned behaviours?**
   Take the Realise2 online strengths assessment at www.strengths2020.com

2. **Do you want to find out more about strengths generally?**
   Access the resources and materials including free downloads, research reports, strengths videos and strengths tips, available at www.strengths2020.com.

3. **Do you want to become a Strengths Practitioner?**
   Sign up for one of the Strengths Practitioner Programmes we run, to learn about Realise2 and its applications — in coaching, development, management, and training — in more depth. Visit us at www.cappeu.com for more details.

4. **Do you want to apply strengths in your people management practices?**
   Engage with CAPP to take strengths further in your organisation. We work in the areas of recruitment and selection, performance management, talent and development, engagement and well-being, and re-organisation and outplacement. For more information, visit us at www.cappeu.com.

For more information:
CAPP — www.cappeu.com
Strengths2020 — www.strengths2020.com

9 781906 366094